Jürgen Beyerer, Alexey Pak (Eds.)

**Proceedings of the 2012 Joint Workshop of
Fraunhofer IOSB and Institute for Anthropomatics,
Vision and Fusion Laboratory**

Karlsruher Schriften zur Anthropomatik
Band 13
Herausgeber: Prof. Dr.-Ing. Jürgen Beyerer

Lehrstuhl für Interaktive Echtzeitsysteme
Karlsruher Institut für Technologie

Fraunhofer-Institut für Optronik, Systemtechnik und
Bildauswertung IOSB Karlsruhe

Eine Übersicht über alle bisher in dieser Schriftenreihe erschienenen Bände finden Sie am Ende des Buchs.

Proceedings of the 2012 Joint Workshop of Fraunhofer IOSB and Institute for Anthropomatics, Vision and Fusion Laboratory

Edited by
Jürgen Beyerer
Alexey Pak

 Scientific Publishing

Impressum

Karlsruher Institut für Technologie (KIT)
KIT Scientific Publishing
Straße am Forum 2
D-76131 Karlsruhe
www.ksp.kit.edu

KIT – Universität des Landes Baden-Württemberg und
nationales Forschungszentrum in der Helmholtz-Gemeinschaft

KIT Scientific Publishing 2013
Print on Demand

ISSN 1863-6489
ISBN 978-3-86644-988-6

Preface

In 2012, the annual joint workshop of the Fraunhofer Institute of Optronics, System Technologies and Image Exploitation (IOSB) and the Vision and Fusion Laboratory (IES) of the Institute for Anthropomatics, Karlsruhe Institute of Technology (KIT) has again been hosted by the town of Triberg-Nussbach in Germany.

For a week from July, 22 to 28 the doctoral students of the both institutions delivered extensive reports on the status of their research and participated in thorough discussions on topics ranging from computer vision and world modeling to data fusion and human-machine interaction. Most results and ideas presented at the workshop are collected in this book in the form of detailed technical reports. This volume provides thus a comprehensive and up-to-date overview of the research program of the IES Laboratory and the Fraunhofer IOSB.

The editors thank Yvonne Fischer, Michael Teutsch and the other organizers for their efforts resulting in a pleasant and inspiring atmosphere throughout the week. We would also like to thank the doctoral students for writing and reviewing the technical reports as well as for responding to the comments and the suggestions of their colleagues.

Prof. Dr.-Ing. Jürgen Beyerer
Alexey Pak, PhD

Contents

Deflectometry in Motion   1
Alexey Pak

Review and Outlook for Texture Analysis Methods   11
Markus Vogelbacher

Utilizing Temporal Information for Object Recognition   27
Michael Teutsch

Greedy Planning   39
Masoud Roschani

Underwater Imaging Model   51
Thomas Stephan

On Adaptive Open-World Modeling   61
Achim Kuwertz

Challenges of Position Coding with Thermal Patterns   75
Sebastian Höfer

Towards Mobile Gaze Analysis   85
Jan Hendrik Hammer

Filter Optimization for a CCT Sensor   101
Miro Taphanel

Inverse uncertainty quantification of distributed parameter system   113
Chettapong Janya-anurak

Methods for Multiscale Evaluation of Deflectometric Measurements   127
Mathias Ziebarth

Towards Efficient Deflectometry in Motion

Alexey Pak

Vision and Fusion Laboratory
Institute for Anthropomatics
Karlsruhe Institute of Technology (KIT), Germany
alexey.pak@ies.uni-karlsruhe.de

Technical Report IES-2012-01

Abstract:
Despite years of research, the reliable shape reconstruction of highly specular objects is still a largely unsolved problem, especially for complex objects or worse-than-ideal observation conditions. In this report, we elaborate
on a novel multi-view specular reconstruction method based on the consistency of normal vector maps (NVMs). In particular, this algorithm is applicable to complex moving objects, where most "standard" techniques fail. We
start by demonstrating how NVMs represent the specular reflection data, then
re-formulate the reconstruction problem in terms of an energy functional to
be optimized. Finally, we suggest an efficient solution of the problem as a
modification of the probabilistic voxel carving approach.

1 Introduction

In the recent years the tools to reconstruct 3D textured surfaces from multiple
views (or video streams) have become powerful enough to enable numerous applications in industry and research (see e.g. [Liu11] for a review of the current
techniques and applications). Similar solutions for surfaces exhibiting strong specularity would also have found multiple immediate applications: for instance, car
producers would welcome an objective computer vision-based method to inspect
the finished car bodies as they move through a light tunnel – a task that is presently
done by humans.

However, the approaches that appear in the literature require very demanding measurement conditions or make strong assumptions about the reconstructed surfaces.
In particular, a deflectometric inspection requires that the object is fixed with respect to the camera and the calibrated pattern generator during multiple pattern

exposures. In addition, one also needs some "regularization", i.e. external information about the location of the surface; the fusion of multiple measurements is also non-trivial [WMHB09].

Nevertheless, the state-of-the-art deflectometric measurements now compete in accuracy with interferometry [FOKH12] due to extreme sensitivity of specular reflection to surface gradient changes. The ultimate solution would combine the flexibility of triangulation-based methods with the accuracy of deflectometry, possibly incorporating (but not crucially depending on) any additional information not contained in the camera images.

An alternative method of fringe reflectometry [HNA11] operates with single shots, and thus applies also to dynamic scenes. However, the reconstructed surfaces may only slightly deviate from a plane, and the scene geometry cannot be independently determined from the reconstruction itself. In addition, the method as described by Huang et al. is sensitive only to a narrow band of surface feature scales, which may potentially limit its general applicability.

In another recent work [WASS12], a moving surface is scanned by a laser ray constrained to a plane. The rays reflected from the surface draw a line on a diffusive screen, which is observed by a camera. The surface is reconstructed from the shape analysis of that line. While reportedly fast and accurate, this method also needs regularization, and utilizes in each camera snapshot only a fraction of the information potentially available in a series of deflectometric images.

Finally, the method of voxel carving based on normal vector consistency [BS03] enjoys potentially rather broad applicability. The volume containing the reconstructed object is divided into small regions (voxels), which can be occupied or empty. The camera images are processed to identify the (distorted) reflections of the unique point neighbourhoods of the calibrated pattern screen. The found correspondences then are used to reconstruct possible normal vectors of a surface under the assumption that it pass through a given voxel; finally, the voxels with incompatible reconstructed normals are labeled as empty.

While simple to implement, this method has several weak points. First, a sufficiently curved surface may distort the point neighborhoods so strongly that a reliable detection becomes impossible, and the resulting set of sparse constraints becomes too small. Second, as the authors of the above reference mention, the reconstruction accuracy depends sharply on the tolerance for normal vector deviations per voxel. This parameter is set globally and requires careful fine-tuning. Third, the naive voxel carving implemented in that paper gives no respect to voxel occlusions that are more than possible for any real-life objects.

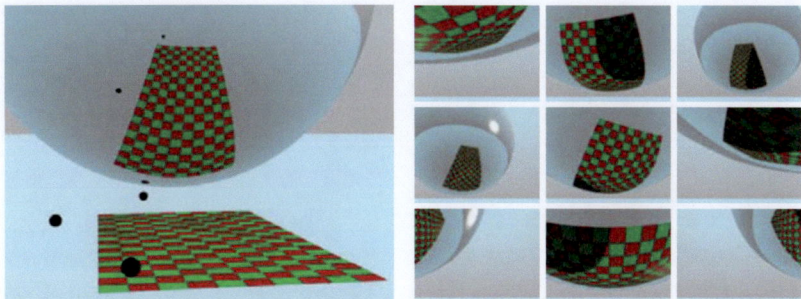

(a) Simulated scene with the studied object (specular sphere) at the initial position, three cameras (marked with the black spheres), and the pattern screen.

(b) Images from the three cameras (one row per camera) corresponding to the three different object positions (one position per column).

Figure 2.1: Sample deflectometric setup with the object, pattern, and the cameras.

Our approach, first suggested in Ref. [Pak12] and further developed in this report, also employs voxel carving, but builds on a more general consistency condition. Instead of a single normal vector per voxel, we consider a set of all vectors consistent with multiple observations. The (non-unique) identification of color-coded pattern areas allows to build such sets without reliance on the fragile neighborhood analysis. Invalid voxels then receive inconsistent observations that lead to the empty set. The cones of candidate normal vector directions may be stored as e.g. two-dimensional maps on a unit sphere, and one effectively has to operate with two-dimensional binary images, as opposed to single vectors as in the method of Bonfort et al.

2 Normal vector maps

In order to discuss the construction of NVMs, we consider the synthetic scene in Fig. 2.1(a). We simulate several object positions, and capture (render) images from the three cameras (marked by black spheres) such as in Fig. 2.1(b). We assume that the position of the object's bounding box is available[1], and thus each observation also includes the camera projection parameters, and camera and pattern screen position and orientation with respect to the object.

---

[1] In a realistic measurement, this information can be obtained by e.g. tracking non-specular markers applied on or co-moving with the object; another possibility would be to treat these coordinates probabilistically and determine them by maximizing the likelihood. We postpone the detailed study of this question to further publications.

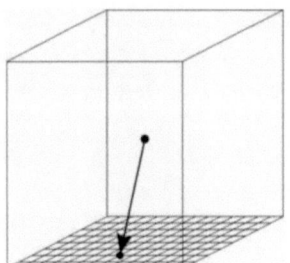

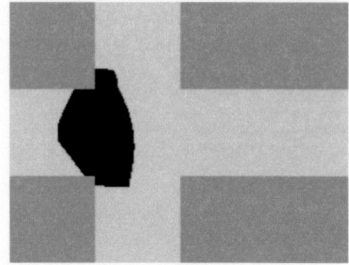

Figure 2.2: Rasterized cube surface as the parameterization of solid angles as viewed from the center of the cube.

Figure 2.3: Unfolded normal vector map. Black pixels mark the allowed, light gray – the excluded directions.

In order to perform voxel carving, one has to model the observations of small volumes of space. For simplicity, in all further examples we limit ourselves to considering the voxels being axis-aligned cuboids (more complex shapes, needed by complex voxel-carving algorithms, can be treated similarly).

Given a voxel, one first scans the camera pixels where it projects and identifies the observed pixel colors with those projected by the pattern generator. Discarding the underexposed (black) and the overexposed (white) pixels, the pattern colors can most easily be identified in the HSV-space (for hue-saturation-value) by comparing the hue component. Since the rendered images are anti-aliased, it is also important to properly attribute the transition pixels with intermediate color values.

The following step is to build the cones of the normal vectors compatible with the observation. Since the end result is an arbitrarily shaped "fan of rays", we parameterize it by rasterizing the complete 4π solid angle on a unit cube surface, as in Fig. 2.2. Each pixel on each face of the cube corresponds to a narrow cone originating from the center of the cube, and requires one bit of storage for labeling it either "allowed" or "excluded". Given sufficiently high resolution, the inhomogeneous density of the covered solid angle per pixel over the planar face is not important. In our implementation, each cube face contains 64x64 binary pixels (one bit per pixel), so that the complete net requires 3072 bytes.

In order to visualize the maps of the allowed directions, we unfold the cube surface into a net and interpret is as a planar image, such as in Fig. 2.3. The example in that figure displays a single cone of the allowed vectors that is directed primarily downwards (i.e. in the negative z direction), is slightly tilted forward (in the positive x direction), and does not intersect with the back and the top cube faces.

Let us consider the situation when the voxel color is identified as originating from some region of the pattern. Having chosen a point $\vec{V}$ inside the voxel, and a point

$\vec{P}$ on the corresponding area in the pattern, the reflection condition is

$$\vec{n} \sim \frac{\vec{C} - \vec{V}}{\left|\vec{C} - \vec{V}\right|} + \frac{\vec{P} - \vec{V}}{\left|\vec{P} - \vec{V}\right|},$$

where $\vec{C}$ is the camera location. We may now add the unit normal vector $\vec{n}$ to the map (i.e. set the corresponding pixel on one of the cube faces to true), and continue with some other combination of $\vec{V}$ and $\vec{P}$.

The above strategy is not extremely efficient and can be improved in multiple ways. We have implemented algorithms that work efficiently when the pattern contains a few uniformly filled polygons; depending on the pattern complexity, the final speedup compared to the above "naive" filling may be $\mathcal{O}(10^3 - 10^4)$, the details to be reported in a following publication.

3 Single-voxel simulation

It is easy to see that the bitwise AND-fusion of NVMs for several views leaves only the directions that satisfy all conditions simultaneously. In Fig. 3.1 we present a few camera images and the corresponding NVMs, generated by the sequential AND-fusion for a single voxel. The frame in Fig. 3.1(a) is the first in the sequence, and thus the cumulative and the instantaneous NVMs are identical. In Fig. 3.1(a) and 3.1(b), the voxel image contains pixels of both pattern colors, which means that the reflected rays may have originated anywhere inside the entire pattern screen. In this case, we only include the normals compatible with the reflection towards the pattern.

In Fig. 3.1(c), the voxel contains one recognized and some unrecognized colors (but not the second pattern color); the corresponding pattern areas have to be excluded from the fully populated NVM. Finally, in Fig. 3.1(d) only unknown colors are observed. All these situations contribute to the cumulative NVMs, which in the end (i.e. after the fourth scene) matches quite closely the ground truth (the arrow endpoint).

A simulation of a single voxel tracked over 200 scenes, where each camera image has the dimensions of 512 x 384 pixels, takes a few seconds on a laptop PC. The memory requirements are relatively modest: each NVM occupies 3072 bytes, and one needs one current and one cumulative NVM per voxel.

The simplest reconstruction as in this example contains multiple opportunities for parallelization. Each voxel and each scene can be processed independently; color

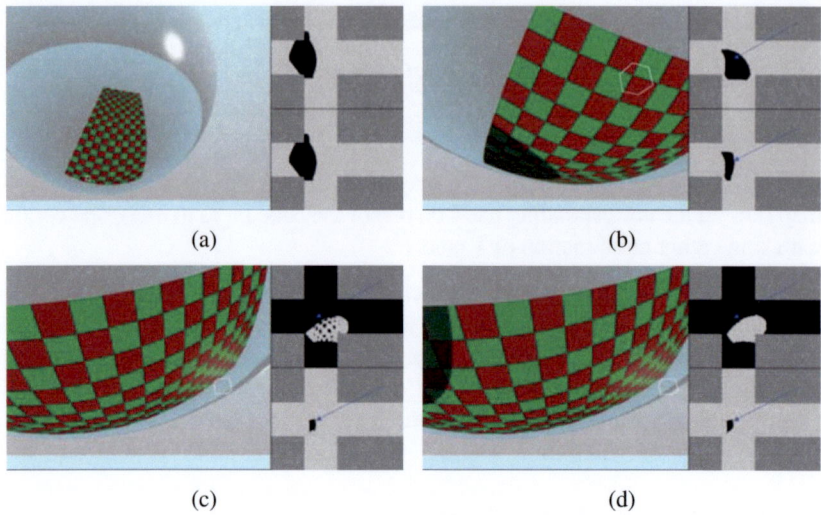

(a)   (b)

(c)   (d)

Figure 3.1: Four subsequent (but not consecutive) steps from the reconstruction sequence for a single voxel that does enclose real surface. The voxel is denoted on the camera image with the white outline. In each frame, the upper NVM represents the instantaneous, the lower – the cumulative limitation of the recovered normal vectors for the voxel. The arrows indicate the locations of the actual normal (i.e. the ground truth). Frames (a) and (b) are taken with the first camera (the nearest to the observer in Fig. 2.1(a)), (c) and (d) – from the second camera (the leftmost camera in Fig. 2.1(a)).

identification can be done off-line and re-used for different voxels; polygon-filling and NVM fusion can be run on graphic cards etc.

4   Results of naive voxel carving

As discussed above, a sequence of camera observations in principle contains all the necessary information to recover the shape and the position of the object. However, the actual reconstruction results from a limited sequence depend strongly on the details: the voxel size, the chosen pattern, the camera resolution etc. In Fig. 4.1(right) we present the final NVMs corresponding to a single layer of voxels inside a small volume enclosing the boundary of a sphere (Fig. 4.1, left). The NVM fusion was performed "naively" as described above, and the volume and observations were chosen in order to avoid possible occlusions.

Approximately half of the voxels in the chosen layer lay inside the sphere or on the surface, the other half is outside. In the ideal situation, only a subset of NVMs in the upper-left corner of the resulting grid would remain non-empty. In reality, the remaining cones of normal vectors in the complementary region are narrow but non-zero, and the exclusion power of NVMs per se happens to be insufficient to reliably distinguish between the occupied and the empty voxels.

There exists several possible remedies to this situation. First, we may notice that the camera positions were too close to each other to reliably determine the distance to the object. A wider stereo base would solve this problem, but it would also give rise to occlusions. In a naive carving scheme, a voxel's NVM would then be affected by the occluded views, resulting in the wrong reconstruction.

Employing a priori information could also improve the result. For example, continuous objects tend to have similar occupancy values for the adjacent points. Similarly, smooth surfaces have strong correlations between the normal vectors at the close surface locations.

5   Probabilistic voxel carving

In order to merge the specular information with the a priori knowledge, one would ideally use some sort of a probabilistic framework. The approach that we chose as a model has been successfully employed in the state-of-the-art voxel carving tools, reconstructing diffuse objects [Liu11]. Below we re-formulate our problem following the notation of the above reference and suggest the possible solutions.

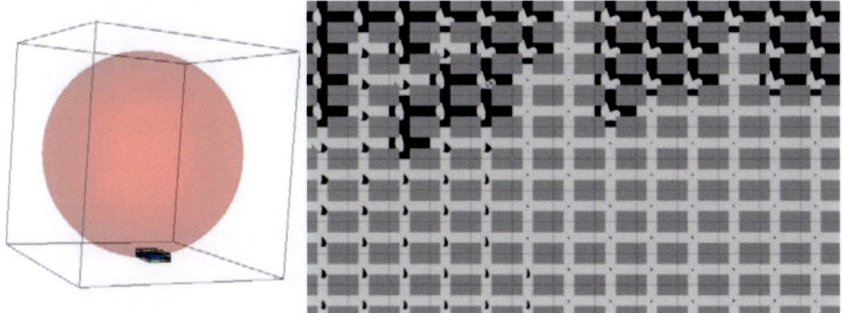

Figure 4.1: Right: location of voxelized volume and a "slice" of reconstructed voxels; left: resulting NVMs reconstructed from a sequence of 200 observations.

Let us consider a set $X = \{x_i\}$ of voxels, $i = 1, ..., N$. Each voxel is placed at position $\vec{r} = (x, y, z)$ and features the binary occupancy $o \in \{0, 1\}$ and the unit normal vector $\hat{n}$, i.e. $x_i = (\vec{r}_i, o_i, \hat{n}_i)$. The reconstruction then can be reformulated as an optimization problem:

$$X^* = \arg\min_X E(X), \tag{5.1}$$

where the energy functional $E(X)$ is

$$E(X) = \sum_i E_u(x_i) + \sum_{i,j} E_p(x_i, x_j) + \sum_{r \in R} E_R(\{x\}_r). \tag{5.2}$$

Here the second sum is performed over the pairs of the adjacent voxels, and $\{x\}_r$ in the last sum denotes the ordered set of voxels traversed by the ray r taken from the set of all rays R.

The unit energy E_u describes our a priori preference for a specific occupancy/normal vector combination in each point in space. In the simplest form, it may simply encode the desired fraction of the volume occupied by the object:

$$E_u^{\text{simple}}(x_i) = w_u(1 - o_i).$$

A more sophisticated function can encode a detailed information such as a CAD-model or a suitable simple basic shape.

The pairwise energy E_p describes the correlation between the two voxels. If the normal vector is not taken into consideration, only the correlation between the two occupancies remains:

$$E_p^{\text{simple}}(x_i, x_j) = w_p(o_i - o_j)^2 \|\vec{r}_i - \vec{r}_j\|^{-1}.$$

Likewise, a more complicated function would also involve normal-occupancy and normal-normal interactions.

The a priori terms give the optimization some "guidelines", and one may discuss the optimal functional form or the strength coefficients. However, the most interesting term in Eq. (5.2) is the ray energy E_R, which we suggest to take as follows:

$$E_R(\{x\}_r) = \min_{\hat{n} \in \text{NVM}(r, \vec{r}_i)} \|\hat{n}_{i^*} - \hat{n}\|^2. \tag{5.3}$$

The index i^* here denotes the first occupied voxel on the ray. For example, given the voxels on the ray $\{x\}_r = (x_{i_1}, ..., x_{i_K})$, i^* is defined as

$$i^* = \begin{cases} i_1, & o_{i_1} = 1 \\ i_2, & o_{i_1} = 0, o_{i_2} = 1 \\ ... & ... \end{cases}.$$

The minimum in Eq. (5.3) is taken over all normals consistent with the color of the ray r at the position of the observed voxel $\vec{r}_{i*}$, or over the members of the set of directions allowed by the NVM, denoted as $\mathrm{NVM}(r, \vec{r}_{i*})$. Finding this minimum itself is an optimization problem, with the minimum energy of zero reached when the current normal vector is inside the allowed set, and growing quadratically with the distance to this set otherwise.

The optimization of the complete model in Eq. (5.1) (equivalent to maximum a posteriori probability inference in a higher-order Markov random field) is a formidable task, since the search space includes N discrete and $2N$ continuous parameters. However, the method of "deep belief propagation" of Ref. [Liu11] gives a recipe to efficiently compute the messages from the ray factors to variables, which allows it to successfully find solutions with tens of millions of voxels (for photo-consistency reconstruction). Our model has a very similar structure and we expect similar performance benefits also in the (explicitly non-linear) formulation of Eq. (5.2). As of writing this report, the development of the reconstruction program is still underway.

6 Conclusion

This report summarizes the current status of the suggested method of shape reconstruction from multiple views with the help of NVMs. We outline the basic ideas behind the algorithm, identify the weaknesses of a naive implementation, and suggest the mathematical grounds for the general probabilistic framework. As a solution method, we suggest to use the "deep belief propagation" algorithm that has been shown to successfully perform in similar problems.

Bibliography

[BS03]   Thomas Bonfort and Peter Sturm. Voxel carving for specular surfaces. Proc. 9th IEEE International Conference on Computer Vision (ICCV '03), pages 691–696, 2003.

[FOKH12] Christian Faber, Evelyn Olesch, Roman Krobot, and Gerd Häusler. Deflectometry challenges interferometry: the competition gets tougher! Proc. SPIE 8493, Interferometry XVI: Techniques and Analysis, pages 84930R–84930R–15, 2012.

[HNA11]   L. Huang, C. S. Ng, and A. K. Asundi. Dynamic three-dimensional sensing for specular surface with monoscopic fringe reflectometry. Optics Express, 19:12809–12814, 2011.

[Liu11]   Shubao Liu. Statistical Inverse Ray Tracing for Image-Based 3-d Modeling. PhD thesis, Brown University, 2011.

[Pak12]   Alexey Pak. Recovering shapes of specular objects in motion via normal vector map consistency. Proc. SPIE 8493, Interferometry XVI: Techniques and Analysis, pages 84930T–84930T–8, 2012.

[WASS12]   R. D. Wedowski, G. A. Atkinson, M. L. Smith, and L. N. Smith. A system for the dynamic industrial inspection of specular freeform surfaces. *Optics and Lasers in Engineering*, 50:632–644, 2012.

[WMHB09]   S. Werling, M. Mai, M. Heizmann, and J. Beyerer. Inspection of specular and partially specular surfaces. *Metrology and Measurement Systems*, 16, 2009.

Review and Outlook for Texture Analysis Methods

Markus Vogelbacher

Vision and Fusion Laboratory
Institute for Anthropomatics
Karlsruhe Institute of Technology (KIT), Germany
markus.vogelbacher@kit.edu

Technical Report IES-2012-02

Abstract:

The description and analysis of textures is a widely discussed topic. Different methods have already been developed but there are still a lot of opportunities to develop new approaches. For this reason, in this report at first an overview of the standard methods for the analysis of textures is given. Based on that, new ideas and opportunities are presented which extend these methods but also represent totally new approaches. In the field of structural-statistical textures the change in the structural arrangement scheme is described analogously to the modulation of signals in communications technology. A basic fundament is the representation of an image signal by a two-dimensional extended Fourier series whose parameters can be obtained using unmodulated texture primitives. Another subject is the determination of parameters in the modeling of textures using AR-models. This estimate is carried out using the Support Vector Regression (SVR) and, thus, offers an alternative to the in the field of texture analysis widely used Least-Square (LS) and Maximum-Likelihood (ML) estimation methods. In the field of optical inspection of textiles an approach will be introduced, which enables the assessment of tissue properties and the detection of errors. The assessment is not based on the derivation of features from the methods of texture analysis, but uses the possibilities of the image acquisition by a variable illumination.

1 Introduction

For the term *texture* there is no clear definition. The word comes from the Latin *textura* and literally means *tissue*. Textures, e.g., on surfaces, are very familiar to us from everyday life and often they are described by various adjectives such as

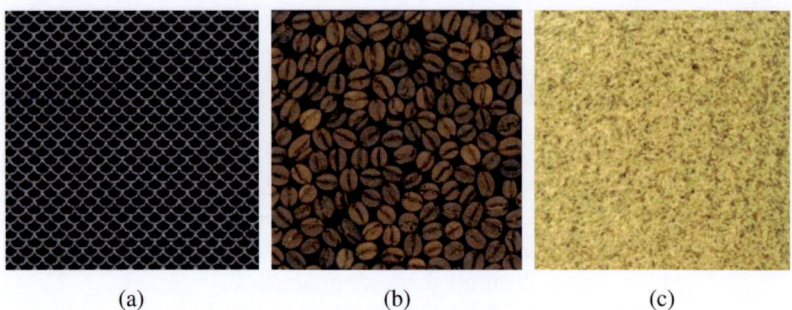

(a)   (b)   (c)

Figure 1.1: Examples of texture types: (a) structural, (b) structural-statistical, (c) statistical.

coarse, fine, grainy, directed, wavy, etc.. Also in image processing the classification, segmentation, modeling, and fault detection of textures is an important part of the inspection and evaluation of surfaces.

As already mentioned, there is no generally accepted definition for texture, but basically, any two-dimensional structure with certain deterministic or statistical regularities can be characterized as such. According to this definition, a basic separation of textures can be made into the following types (Fig. 1.1):

- Structural texture type

- Structural-statistical texture type

- Statistical texture type

A structural texture type can thereby be described by a given elementary sample, which is also known as texture primitive or texel, arranged at a fixed local arrangement scheme. If the primitive or the arrangement scheme is subject to certain stochastic variations, we speak of a structural-statistical texture type. If none of these is recognizable, e.g., the texture is a sample function of a random process, it is seen as statistical texture type. Basically, it can be stated that in the transition from the statistical to structural-statistical and to structural texture type the knowledge about the texture increases.

The various types of texture can be characterized by various methods. The introduction to this standard methods of texture analysis is carried out in Section 2. Section 3 deals with two approaches: the first introduces a way of describing/modeling structural-statistical texture types and the second offers an alternative to the existing methods for parameter estimation at autoregressive (AR)-models.

Another approach to assess semi-finished textile surfaces is part of Section 4. The tissue properties are assessed and errors are detected by using the properties of the textured surface even at the image acquisition. A summary and outlook are given in Section 5.

2 Overview and Insight into the Methods of Texture Analysis

The separation into different texture types shows the diversity in the evaluation of textures that must be considered. A single procedure for texture analysis, which allows an assessment of all the properties of all types of texture, does not exist. Rather the methods are based on the existing texture type. Below, some classic texture analysis approaches are presented, which can be divided into the following categories:

- Statistical methods

- Structural/spectral methods

- Use of special masks

- Texture models

This methods can be used for classification, segmentation, or defect detection.

2.1 Statistical Methods

To represent texture, various properties are determined mainly describing the spatial dependence of the gray values within a particular neighborhood. With these properties in further steps, e.g., classification can be made.

As the visual perception of a texture by humans are strongly dominated by differences in the statistics of the first and second order and differences in higher order statistics are perceived very rarely, histogram properties such as the mean, the variance, the autocorrelation function, or the edge density are used for the evaluation of a texture. The measurement of these properties in a particular window which is slided over a texture can, e.g., enable the segmentation of a texture or the detection of defects by considering the deviations of the properties depending on the window position.

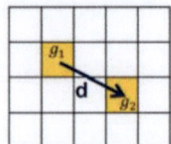

Figure 2.1: Displacement **d** for the determination of the gray level co-occurrence matrix.

A process which is concerned with the assessment of the neighborhood of a pixel involves setting up a gray level co-occurrence matrix (GLCM) [HSD73, Bey11]. The gray values of two pixels $g_1 = g(\mathbf{x})$ and $g_2 = g(\mathbf{x} + \mathbf{d})$ are considered, which have a certain displacement **d** to each other (Fig. 2.1).

The elements of the GLCM $\mathbf{C_d}$ can be determined as follows:

$$c_{\mathbf{d},ij} = |\{\mathbf{x}|g(\mathbf{x}) = i, g(\mathbf{x} + \mathbf{d}) = j, \forall \mathbf{x}, \mathbf{x} + \mathbf{d} \in \Omega\}|$$

The element $c_{\mathbf{d},ij}$ describes the number of pixels $\mathbf{x}$ in the domain Ω of the image with $g_1 = g(\mathbf{x}) = i$ and $g_2 = g(\mathbf{x} + \mathbf{d}) = j$. An example of the determination of such a GLCM is shown in Fig. 2.2.

Since the determination of GLCMs compares values of pixel pairs they belong to statistics of second order. By normalizing the matrix by

$$\mathbf{C_d^{norm}} = \frac{\mathbf{C_d}}{\mathbf{1}^T \mathbf{C_d} \mathbf{1}},$$

this can be interpreted as estimation for the second order composite likelihood.

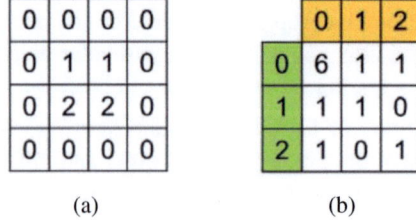

(a)   (b)

Figure 2.2: Example of the determination of a GLCM with $\mathbf{d} = (1\ 0)^T$: (a) starting image $g(\mathbf{x})$, (b) co-occurrence matrix $\mathbf{C_d}$ (green column corresponds to the gray value at the point $\mathbf{x}$ and orange line corresponds to the gray value at the point $\mathbf{x} + \mathbf{d}$).

m_1	m_2	m_3
m_8	m_0	m_4
m_7	m_6	m_5

Figure 2.3: Local Binary Pattern: defining the neighborhood m_1 to m_8 for central pixel m_0.

To use the GLCM to analyse textures, various features such as the Haralick-features [Har79] can be derived:

- Energy:

$$\mathbf{1}^{\mathrm{T}} \left[c_{\mathbf{d},ij}^2 \right] \mathbf{1}$$

- Entropy:

$$-\sum_i \sum_j c_{\mathbf{d},ij} \, \mathrm{ld}(c_{\mathbf{d},ij})$$

- Contrast:

$$\sum_i \sum_j |i - j|^a \, c_{\mathbf{d},ij}^b \quad \text{(typically } a = 2,\, b = 1)$$

- Other features: maximum, homogeneity, inverse difference moment, correlation [Har79].

Another method, which attracts also the comparison of the gray values of a pixel pair, is called Local Binary Pattern (LBP) [WH89]. The gray values of pixels that are within a certain distance from a central pixel are considered (Fig. 2.3).

A comparison of gray values delivers a binary encoding for the pixel area. For the considered neighborhood of Fig. 2.3 the result is:

$$LBP(m_0) = \sum_{i=1}^{8} \kappa(m_i) 2^{i-1}, \quad \kappa(m_i) = \begin{cases} 1, & m_i \geq m_0 \\ 0, & \text{else} \end{cases}$$

Evaluating for example histograms of LBPs enables the assessment of a texture.

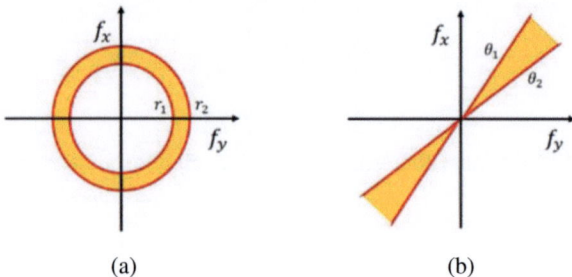

(a)   (b)

Figure 2.4: (a) Ring and (b) Wedge filter to select specific frequencies in the periodogram.

2.2 Structural/Spectral Methods

The analysis of structural textures is based on the detection of the texture primitive and the arrangement scheme. The determination of the primitive or the size of the primitive can be derived from various properties such as GLCM, the autocorrelation function or using the Renyi entropy [GP03]. In most cases an accurate determination of the primitive is very difficult. The analysis of the arrangement scheme can be performed using the periodogram/Fourier transform, so that a determination of the frequency and the orientation of the texture is possible.

For most analysis, a detailed consideration of a certain frequency range is needed. This can be achieved by using so called Ring/Wedge filters [RH99], which put the focus on frequencies between two radii or within a certain angle (Fig. 2.4).

For the detection of structural features other transformations such as the Hough or Radon transform can be used as well. If the primitive and the arrangement scheme is known, the texture can be completely recovered from it.

2.3 Use of Special Masks

One way to assess textures is the use of heuristically derived masks. These are included in the texture energy measure by Laws [Law80] and can describe properties such as level, edge, spot, wave, and ripple. In this context, the required convolution kernels can have different length. As an example the convolution kernels of length five are listed. The designation of the convolution kernels refers to the first letter of each property.

$$\mathbf{l}_5 = \begin{pmatrix} 1 & 4 & 6 & 4 & 1 \end{pmatrix}^{\mathrm{T}}$$
$$\mathbf{e}_5 = \begin{pmatrix} -1 & -2 & 0 & 2 & 1 \end{pmatrix}^{\mathrm{T}}$$
$$\mathbf{s}_5 = \begin{pmatrix} -1 & 0 & 2 & 0 & -1 \end{pmatrix}^{\mathrm{T}}$$
$$\mathbf{r}_5 = \begin{pmatrix} 1 & -4 & 6 & -4 & 1 \end{pmatrix}^{\mathrm{T}}$$
$$\mathbf{w}_5 = \begin{pmatrix} 1 & -2 & 6 & 2 & -1 \end{pmatrix}^{\mathrm{T}}$$

By calculating the dyadic product of two convolution kernels with desired properties the so called Laws matrices are obtained. The convolution of a gray-scale image with these Laws matrices and then calculating the resulting image energies allows the classification of different textures.

2.4 Texture Models

The description of an existing texture by using a model can be tackled by different approaches. Firstly, a texture can be described by a fractal model. Accordingly, the texture is treated as a structure that consists of non-overlapping and reduced copies of itself. The measurement of the self-similarity in concrete the fractal dimension

$$D = \frac{\log(N_r)}{\log(\frac{1}{r})}$$

delivers a characteristic of the texture [PGS06]. N_r denotes the number of copies of the non-overlapping structure reduced by a factor r.

A widely used model for textures is given by Markov Random Fields (MRF). A statistical dependence of the gray value of a pixel to the gray values of its neighborhood is produced [CJ83]. The choice of the neighborhood is a very important variable for the quality of the model output.

The autoregressive (AR)-model [MJ92] is an instance of the MRF model. A detailed description is given in Section 3.

3   Possible Enhancements of Existing Texture Analysis Methods

3.1 Texture Modulation

The description or the designation of a model for a structural-statistical texture type is a hardly studied area in the field of texture analysis. Below, an approach which interprets the structural-statistical texture as modulation of a structural texture is presented. The structural texture is modeled by using a two-dimensional Fourier series. The local changes of the arrangement scheme, which create the structural-statistical texture, will be considered by a modulation term.

The basis of this idea lies in the communications technology. A signal $x(t) = a_0 \cos(2\pi f_0 t + \varphi_0)$ can be affected by an amplitude (AM) $x_{AM}(t)$ or frequency modulation (FM) $x_{FM}(t)$. The modulating signal used in this case is denoted by $v(t)$. AM and FM can be described as follows:

$$x_{AM}(t) = [a_0 + a_1 v(t)] \cos(2\pi f_0 t + \varphi_0),$$
$$x_{FM}(t) = a_0 \cos(2\pi f_0 t + \Delta\Omega\, V(t) + \varphi_0),$$

$$\text{with } V(t) = \int_0^t v(t')\, dt' \text{ and } \Delta\Omega = \text{frequency deviation.}$$

By calculating the analytical signal $x_{AM}^+(t)$ or $x_{FM}^+(t)$ with the Hilbert transform

$$\mathcal{H}\left\{\cos(2\pi f_0 t)\right\} = \sin(2\pi f_0 t),$$
$$x_{AM}^+(t) = x_{AM}(t) + j\mathcal{H}\left\{x_{AM}\right\} = [a_0 + a_1 v(t)]\, e^{j(2\pi f_0 t + \varphi_0)},$$
$$x_{FM}^+(t) = x_{FM}(t) + j\mathcal{H}\left\{x_{FM}\right\} = a_0\, e^{j(2\pi f_0 t + \Delta\Omega\, V(t) + \varphi_0)},$$

and by using the complex envelope

$$s(t) = \frac{1}{\sqrt{2}}\, x^+(t)\, e^{j2\pi f_0 t},$$
$$\text{for } x_{AM}^+(t): \quad |s(t)| = |a_0 + a_1 v(t)|,$$
$$\text{for } x_{FM}^+(t): \quad Im\left\{\ln s(t)\right\} = \Delta\Omega\, V(t) + \varphi_0,$$

the modulating signal can be obtained again. Demodulation is possible, too [Kam11].

The idea is in the first step to extend the approach to the modulation of any one-dimensional signal and in the second step for any two-dimensional signal/texture.

In order to determine the analytical signal the simple correspondence to the Hilbert transform of sin and cos is still to be exploited.

With the representation of an arbitrary periodic signal by means of a Fourier series in amplitude-phase-notation a modulation for any one-dimensional signal can be achieved analogously to a simple cos-signal in the communication technology:

$$x(t) = \frac{a_0}{2} + \sum_{n=1}^{\infty} A_n \cos(n2\pi f_0 t - \varphi_n)$$

$$\text{AM:} \quad x_{AM}^{+}(t) = v(t) \left[\frac{a_0}{2} + \sum_{n=1}^{\infty} A_n \, e^{j(n2\pi f_0 t - \varphi_n)} \right]$$

$$\text{FM:} \quad x_{FM}^{+}(t) = \frac{a_0}{2} + \sum_{n=1}^{\infty} A_n \, e^{j(n(2\pi f_0 t + \Delta\Omega \, V(t)) - \varphi_n)}$$

a_0, A_n and φ_n describe the Fourier coefficients of the unmodulated signal.

Just like in the one-dimensional space, every two-dimensional periodic signal or in specific a texture can be expressed by means of a two-dimensional Fourier series. The creation of the analytical signal can be replaced by the direct use of the complex 2D Fourier series:

$$f(x, y) = \sum_{m=-\infty}^{\infty} \sum_{n=-\infty}^{\infty} E_{mn} \, e^{j(m2\pi f_x x + n2\pi f_y y)},$$

$$\text{with } f_x = \frac{1}{T_x}, \, f_y = \frac{1}{T_y} \text{ , and}$$

$$E_{mn} = \frac{1}{T_x T_y} \int_{-T_y}^{T_y} \int_{-T_x}^{T_x} e^{-j(m2\pi f_x x + n2\pi f_y y)} f(x, y) \, dx \, dy.$$

By introducing a modulation term, the modulation of a two-dimensional signal can be described by an extended 2D Fourier series. For example for the frequency modulation:

$$f_{FM}(x, y) = \sum_{m=-\infty}^{\infty} \sum_{n=-\infty}^{\infty} E_{mn} \, e^{j(m(2\pi f_x x + \Delta\Omega_x \, V_x(x)) + n(2\pi f_y y + \Delta\Omega_y \, V_y(y)))},$$

$$\text{with } V_x(x) = \int_{0}^{x} v_x(x') \, dx', \, V_y(y) = \int_{0}^{y} v_y(y') \, dy'.$$

In Fig. 3.1, an example of modeling a 2D-modulated signal is given in which the modulation of the arrangement scheme is known.

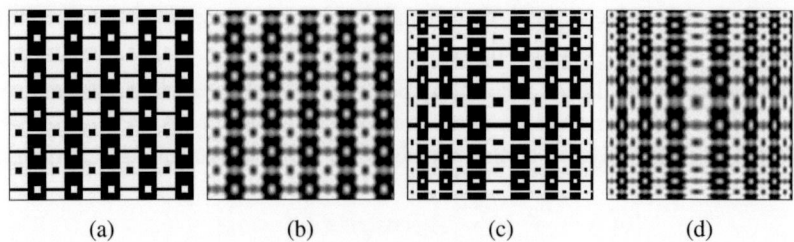

(a)   (b)   (c)   (d)

Figure 3.1: Application of the extended Fourier series to a texture with a known modulated arrangement scheme: (a) unmodulated original texture, (b) model of the extended Fourier series of the unmodulated original texture, (c) modulated original texture, (d) model of the extended Fourier series of the modulated original texture.

It turns out that this approach can represent structural-statistical textures with known modulated arrangement scheme. However, the simple demodulation, as known from the communication technology, is no longer possible. For derivation of the modulating signal from the model of the extended Fourier series, it is necessary to find other methods. Such methods may be derived from similar applications such as the estimation of a time-frequency distribution using the short-time Fourier transform or the Wavelet transform [LT96], the adjusting of the phase of the extended Fourier series with the aid of a phase locked loop, or the use of distribution densities for point fields [SS92]. The possible applications of these various methods must be investigated in further steps. Furthermore, the introduction of a combined x, y-modulation is necessary, since in the previously considered case the modulation is divided into separated x- and y-direction ($V_x(x)$ and $V_y(y)$).

3.2   Alternative Parameter Estimation for AR-Texture Models

AR-models are well-known for the analysis of statistical textures [Bey11]. The intensity at a discrete location g_{mn} can be modeled as follows:

$$g_{mn} = \sum_{(k,l)\in U} a_{kl}\, g_{m-k,n-l} + e_{mn}$$

$$= \mathbf{a}^{\mathrm{T}}\boldsymbol{\gamma}_{mn} + e_{mn},$$

$$\text{with}\quad \mathbf{a} = (...,a_{kl},...)^{\mathrm{T}}\quad \boldsymbol{\gamma}_{mn} = (...,g_{m-k,n-l},...)^{\mathrm{T}}.$$

U describes the causal environment, $|U|$ the order (number of elements in the considered environment), a_{kl} the weighting factors or AR coefficients, and e_{mn} a weakly stationary additive white noise

$$E\{e_{mn}\} = 0, \quad E\{e_{mn}\, e_{m+i,n+j}\} = \sigma^2 \delta_i^0 \delta_j^0.$$

A causal environment in this context means that for a point (m, n) all points $(m - k, n - l)$ in front of it are known. As a result, the modeled image can be determined by recursive implementation of the AR-model. The texture parameters **a** and σ allow the modeling and therefore may be regarded as texture features. An important step in setting up the AR-model represents the parameter estimation of the AR coefficients. In practice, two main methods are used:

- Least-Square (LS)

- Maximum-Likelihood (ML)

The goal of the estimation using LS is to minimize the variance of the prediction error $e_{mn} = g_{mn} - \mathbf{a}^{\mathrm{T}} \boldsymbol{\gamma}_{mn}$. This leads to the following result [JBS09]:

$$Var\{e_{mn}\} = Var\left\{g_{mn} - \mathbf{a}^{\mathrm{T}} \boldsymbol{\gamma}_{mn}\right\} \to Min$$

$$\to \hat{\mathbf{a}} = \left(\sum_{m,n} \boldsymbol{\gamma}_{mn} \boldsymbol{\gamma}_{mn}^{\mathrm{T}}\right)^{-1} \sum_{m,n} \boldsymbol{\gamma}_{mn}\, g_{mn}$$

The ML estimate iteratively calculates the coefficients with $\hat{\mathbf{a}}$ as iteration start and delivers better results than the LS estimation [JBS09].

At this point an alternative variant for parameter estimation of AR-texture models is presented, which is already known from the system technology, namely the estimation using Support Vector Regression (SVR) [RAMRdPC$^+$04]. The aim is to minimize the total error R resulting from the model. The total error R consists of a loss function $\xi^{(*)}$ (for upper and lower bound) and a regularization term for the AR coefficients:

$$R = \frac{1}{2} \|\mathbf{a}\|^2 + C \sum_{i=1}^{N} (\xi_i + \xi_i^*) \qquad N\text{: Number of training data}$$

By introducing the loss function also outliers are allowed similar to the *soft margin* approach at Support Vector Machines (SVM). The constant C controls the balance between the loss function and the regularization term and, thus, the tolerance of outliers. The loss function can be set up differently, a common approach is the ϵ-insensitive loss-function:

$$\xi^{(*)} = \begin{cases} |e_{mn}|, & e_{mn} \geq \epsilon \\ 0, & \text{else} \end{cases}$$

The total error R must be minimized under the constraints:

$$g_{mn} - \mathbf{a}^\mathrm{T}\boldsymbol{\gamma}_{mn} \leq \epsilon + \xi_{mn}$$

$$-g_{mn} + \mathbf{a}^\mathrm{T}\boldsymbol{\gamma}_{mn} \geq \epsilon + \xi_{mn}^*$$

$$\xi^{(*)} \geq 0$$

This optimization problem under constraints can be solved by using Lagrange multipliers $\alpha^{(*)}$. The corresponding Lagrange function is given by:

$$L(a,\alpha,\alpha^*,\eta,\eta^*,\xi,\xi^*) = \frac{1}{2}\|\mathbf{a}\|^2 + C\sum_{i=1}^N (\xi_i + \xi_i^*)$$

$$-\sum_{i=1}^N \alpha_i(-g_i + \mathbf{a}^\mathrm{T}\boldsymbol{\gamma}_i + \epsilon + \xi_i)$$

$$-\sum_{i=1}^N \alpha_i^*(g_i - \mathbf{a}^\mathrm{T}\boldsymbol{\gamma}_i + \epsilon + \xi_i^*) - \sum_{i=1}^N (\eta_i\xi_i + \eta_i^*\xi_i^*)$$

In order to optimize, this equation is minimized with respect to $\mathbf{a}$ and $\xi^{(*)}$, i.e.,

$$\frac{\partial L}{\partial \mathbf{a}} = 0 \quad \text{and} \quad \frac{\partial L}{\partial \xi^{(*)}} = 0.$$

The result of the optimization is:

$$\mathbf{a} = -\sum_{i=1}^N (\alpha_i^* - \alpha_i)\,\boldsymbol{\gamma}_i,$$

$$g_{mn} = -\sum_{i=1}^N (\alpha_i^* - \alpha_i)\,\langle\boldsymbol{\gamma}_i,\boldsymbol{\gamma}_{mn}\rangle,$$

$$\text{with} \quad 0 \leq \alpha_i^{(*)} \leq C.$$

After the insertion of the result of $\mathbf{a}$ to the original equation $L(a,\alpha,\alpha^*,\eta,\eta^*,\xi,\xi^*)$, it can be maximized with respect to the Lagrange multipliers $\alpha^{(*)}$:

$$\frac{\partial L}{\partial \alpha^{(*)}} = 0$$

The $\alpha^{(*)}$ can be obtained and used for estimating the AR coefficients by inserting into the equation for $\mathbf{a}$. This procedure has to be applied for various examples

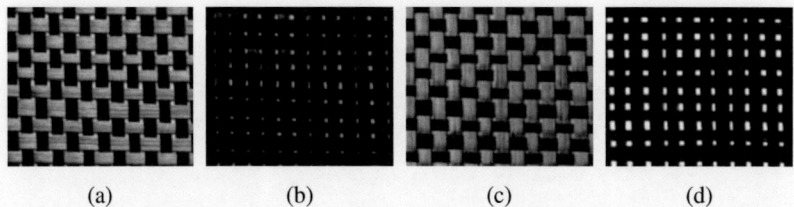

(a)   (b)   (c)   (d)

Figure 4.1: Example for the investigation of a weave structure by variable lighting: (a) perpendicular to weft yarns, (b) not perpendicular to a yarn direction, (c) perpendicular to warp yarns, (d) transmitted light [VWZ12].

from the field of texture analysis and compared with the results of the classical LS and ML estimation methods in further work. Another development potential that has to be examined in this context is the additional introduction of a non-linear extension as known from the classical SVM [SS02].

4 Procedure for Assessing Semi-Finished Textile Surfaces

The visual inspection of textiles is an important part of the texture analysis. Various methods, also presented in Section 2, are used to allow the assessment of the quality of the weave structure or the detection of errors. Examples can be found in [VWZ12].

Also in [VWZ12] an approach is unveiled which goes another way and begins with the image acquisition. Selecting a suitable illumination strategy allows to trace back subsequent steps for assessing the weave structure or the detection of errors to the lighting direction. By taking a series of images, in which the direction of illumination is varied systematically, a reflection characteristic and, thus, an orientation can be assigned to each surface location. The application of such a lighting strategy is based on studies by Lindner, Arigita and Puente León [LAPL05, LPL06].

Examples of a lighting series for weave structure can be seen in Fig. 4.1. The result of a segmentation of the warp and weft yarns as well as the detection of errors in such a series are shown in Fig. 4.2.

The presented weave structure is a structural-statistical texture as desribed in Section 1. Both the texture primitive and the arrangement scheme are variable. The

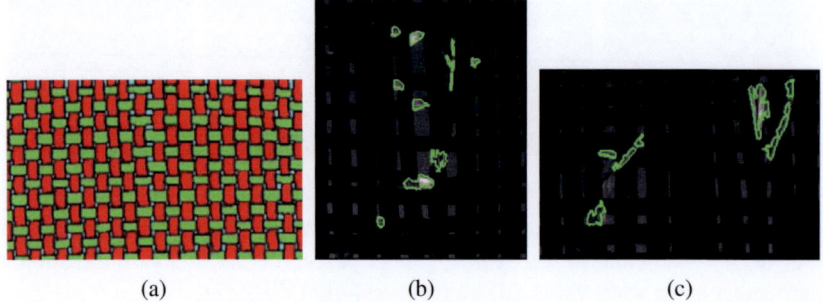

(a)   (b)   (c)

Figure 4.2: Evaluation of a lighting series: (a) segmentation result for yarn spaces (blue), warp (red) and weft threads (green), (b) detection of distortions, (c) detection of damages [VWZ12].

assessment of the degree of variation is not based on a mathematical description (Section 3.1), but on the use of optical properties and following further treatment.

5 Conclusion and Outlook

This report provides an introduction to the basics of texture analysis. Although no universal definition for the term of texture can be given, it was described what a texture is all about and in what types they can be divided to. Moreover, it was shown in an overview which different methods can be used to investigate textures.

In addition to the existing methods new approaches were shown that offer on the one hand the modeling of structural-statistical texture types and on the other an alternative to the estimation techniques used in the field of AR-models for textures. The application, the development, and the resulting advantages and disadvantages of these approaches must be pursued in subsequent studies.

At the end it was shown that texture analysis can not only be carried out by the analysis of image data, but also by the choice of an appropriate lighting strategy and the corresponding information. For the inspection of textiles the approach of using the reflection characteristic has to be further considered.

Bibliography

[Bey11]   J. Beyerer. Lecture: Automatische Sichtprüfung und Bildverarbeitung. *Karlsruher Institut für Technologie, Lehrstuhl für Interaktive Echtzeitsysteme*, 2011.

[CJ83]   G.R. Cross and A.K. Jain. Markov random field texture models. *IEEE Transactions on Pattern Analysis and Machine Intelligence*, PAMI-5(1):25–39, 1983.

[GP03]   S.E. Grigorescu and N. Petkov.   Texture analysis using Renyi's generalized entropies. *International Conference on Image Processing*, 2003.

[Har79]   R.M. Haralick. Statistical and structural approaches to texture. *Proceedings of the IEEE*, 67(5):786 – 804, 1979.

[HSD73]   R.M. Haralick, K. Shanmugam, and I. Dinstein. Textural features for image classification. *IEEE Transactions on Systems, Man and Cybernetics*, SMC-3(6):610–621, 1973.

[JBS09]   M.S. Joshi, P.P. Bartakke, and M.S. Sutaone. Texture representation using autoregressive models. *International Conference on Advances in Computational Tools for Engineering Applications*, pages 386–390, 2009.

[Kam11]   K.D. Kammeyer. *Nachrichtenübertragung*. Vieweg+Teubner Verlag, 2011.

[LAPL05]   C. Lindner, J. Arigita, and F. Puente León. Illumination-based segmentation of structured surfaces in automated visual inspection. In *Society of Photo-Optical Instrumentation Engineers (SPIE) Conference Series*, volume 5856, pages 99–108, 2005.

[Law80]   K. Laws. *Textured Image Segmentation*. PhD thesis, University of Southern California, 1980.

[LPL06]   C. Lindner and F. Puente León. Segmentierung strukturierter Oberflächen mittels variabler Beleuchtung. *Technisches Messen*, 73:200–207, 2006.

[LT96]   P.J. Loughlin and B. Tacer. On the amplitude- and frequency-modulation decomposition of signals. *Journal of the Acoustical Society of America*, 100(3):1594–1601, 1996.

[MJ92]   J. Mao and A.K. Jain. Texture classification and segmentation using multiresolution simultaneous autoregressive models. *Pattern Recognition*, 25(2):173–188, 1992.

[PGS06]   M. Petrou and P. Garcia Sevilla. *Dealing with Texture*. John Wiley & Sons, Ltd, 2006.

[RAMRdPC$^+$04] J.L. Rojo-Alvarez, M. Martinez-Ramon, M. de Prado-Cumplido, A. Artes-Rodriguez, and A.R. Figueiras-Vidal. Support vector method for robust ARMA system identification. *IEEE Transactions on Signal Processing*, 52(1):155–164, 2004.

[RH99]   T. Randen and J.H. Husoy. Filtering for texture classification: A comparative study. *IEEE Transactions on Pattern Analysis and Machine Intelligence*, 21(4):291–310, 1999.

[SS92]   D. Stoyan and H. Stoyan. *Fraktale, Formen, Punktfelder: Methoden der Geometrie-Statistik*. Akademie Verlag, 1992.

[SS02]   B. Schölkopf and A.J. Smola. *Learning with Kernels: Support Vector Machines, Regularization, Optimization, and Beyond*. MIT Press, 2002.

[VWZ12]   M. Vogelbacher, S. Werling, and M. Ziebarth.   Beurteilung textiler Flächenhalbzeuge mittels variabler Beleuchtung. In *Forum Bildverarbeitung*, pages 193–204, 2012.

[WH89]   L. Wang and D.C. He. Texture classification using texture spectrum. *Pattern Recognition*, 23(8):905–910, 1989.

Utilizing Temporal Information in UAV Surveillance Videos for Distant Moving Object Recognition

Michael Teutsch

Vision and Fusion Laboratory
Institute for Anthropomatics
Karlsruhe Institute of Technology (KIT), Germany
teutsch@kit.edu

Technical Report IES-2012-03

Abstract:
Image sequences contain more information than single images due to the temporal context. There are many potential benefits for the automatic analysis of especially distant moving objects in surveillance videos such as temporal noise reduction, track-before-detect, estimating motion information of the camera itself and objects in the scene, or acquiring different appearances of an object for classification. In this report, example approaches are presented for utilizing the temporal information to make the detection, segmentation, and classification of such objects more robust. Using real surveillance datasets, various algorithms for independent motion detection and moving object segmentation are presented and evaluated. Some ideas for considering temporal information for object classification are discussed in a conceptual manner.

1   Introduction

Small and mid-sized Unmanned Aerial Vehicles (UAVs) offer great potential for both wide area surveillance and detailed analysis of objects and regions of interest. Up to now they have been used for military tasks mainly, but applications for public security and safety are becoming more and more popular and helpful. In most cases, UAVs are equipped with imaging sensors such as visual-optical or infrared video cameras and, hence, provide observations with temporal context. Potential applications range from image quality improvement to moving or stationary object detection and recognition, and up to scene analysis and understanding. However, implementing these applications is challenging due to sensor noise, sensor motion, high object distance, or even non-cooperative object behavior. In this report, the focus lies on the detection and analysis of moving objects with standard methods and improving the precision and robustness of these methods by utilizing the temporal information inherent in video data. This approach is well-known for object tracking, of course, but can be used for detection, segmentation, and classification, too. Related work will be presented in the respective sections.

The remainder of the report is geared to the standard image processing chain and, thus, organized as follows: detection is the topic in Section 2, while object segmentation is discussed in Section 3. Some classification concepts are presented in Section 4 and conclusions are given in Section 5.

2   Detection

The aim of detection is to find specific regions, objects or actions of interest in an image or video. Each detection algorithm uses specific features, which describe appearance, action, or behavior. These features must be calculated quickly as the whole image has to be analyzed if no prior knowledge is used. This may become time consuming otherwise. In the follow-up, the focus lies on object detection.

One has to distinguish between object detection and recognition. In case of recognition, the object class is also considered within the detection process and, hence, known after successful detection. This is not the case in pure detection, where objects are found due to specific features but there is no guarantee that a detection is the object of interest. In this case, further processing steps are needed either for better object segmentation or classification.

Popular representatives for object detection are simple or adaptive thresholding if the object is brighter or darker than the background, Maximally Stable Extremal Regions (MSER) [MCUP02], Saliency Maps [IKN98], or the detection of motion in videos either with stable (stationary camera) or dynamic (moving camera) background. Well-known methods for object recognition are using Haar-features with AdaBoost (Viola-Jones) [VJ01], local features (SIFT, SURF) [Low04] and Implicit Shape Models (ISM) [JA11], or Histograms of Oriented Gradients (HOGs) and Sliding Windows [DT05]. Many more methods exist, but the main topic in this section will be the detection of motion with a moving camera, also called *Independent Motion*.

2.1   Independent Motion Detection

Independent Motion Detection is applied to image sequences coming from a moving camera. This is the case for the considered data in this report, which is coming

Figure 2.1: Example scene of a busy inner-city street observed by an UAV.

from a small UAV equipped with a visual-optical camera with a Ground Sampling Distance (GSD) of about 0.34 m/pixel. This means that a standard car covers an area of about 15×5 pixels in the image plane. An example scene with a busy street observed by such UAV can be seen in Fig. 2.1.

Since for a moving camera the whole scene appears to move, independent motion is represented by motion vectors or clusters which are not originating from the stationary background, but from objects like people or cars moving relatively to the background. This also means that motionless objects will not be detected. There are two popular approaches to perform image to image registration, which is the most critical step for camera motion estimation: calculating difference images [KSS$^+$01, XCSH10] or homographies [PSH$^+$06, CLYL11] between subsequent images. In the first one, independent motion appears as clusters, while in the latter one, independent motion shows up as motion vectors which do not fit to the estimated homography. Plane+parallax decompositions with multiview geometric constraints [IA98, YMKC07] do not need to be considered as the evaluation data in this report was recorded from an UAV in higher altitude of about 400 m and a camera directed perpendicularly to the ground.

Both methods were implemented and tested [HEKS08, HEKS10], but the homography-based approach was preferred since it worked better and more robust with the given evaluation data. This basic idea is to detect and track local image features such as KLT features [ST94] for several subsequent images. One motion vector is appearing for each tracked feature and the set of these vectors is used to estimate the homography. This homography estimation works out well if the stationary background covers most textured parts in the image plane. All outlier vectors are assumed to originate from moving objects. One example for this calculation is displayed in Fig. 2.2 which shows the stationary features in red and the moving ones in yellow color. The histogram shows the vector absolutes which correspond to the object velocities. As motion vectors are calculated along more than two consecutive images, even sub-pixel motion is detected.

In difference images those pixels are labeled which differ from each other from image to image after successful registration. Blobs of labeled pixels appear after several consecutive images and can be used for moving object segmentation [KSS$^+$01, XCSH10, CLYL11, RIS10]. However, the big advantage of using

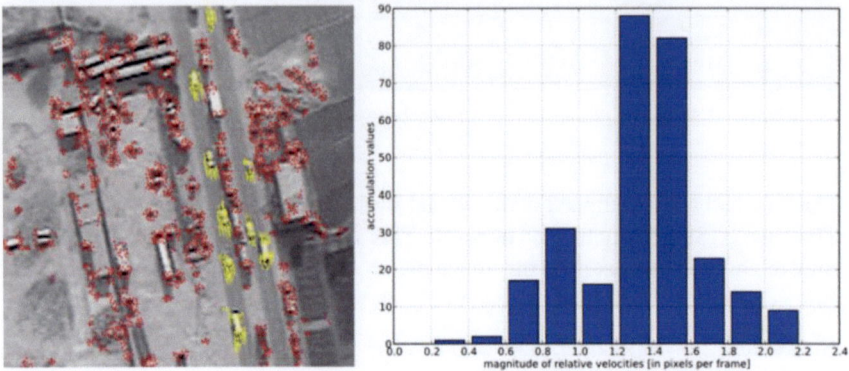

Figure 2.2: Example scene with stationary local features in red and moving local features in yellow. The histogram visualizes the related vector absolutes in pixels.

homographies compared to difference images is that vehicles driving in convoy as seen in the example scene will not grow together.

3   Segmentation

Independent motion is detected on feature level. To analyze an object, it first has to be detected as a whole. This is the aim of object segmentation. Common approaches are clustering of motion pixels in difference images [CLYL11, XCSH10, KSS+01, RIS10] with optional morphological closing [YSM08], background modeling [PSH+06], Graph-Cuts [ICS+10], or Active Contour Models [Zha05].

An easy and for many scenes sufficient solution is the clustering of moving local features based on low spatial distance and similar motion vector direction and absolute. Problems occur when many different objects fulfill all of these criteria. This is the case for vehicles driving in convoy for example and leads to under-segmentation as seen in Fig. 2.3. Big and not well textured vehicles such as the bus in Fig. 2.3 can even lead to over-segmentation.

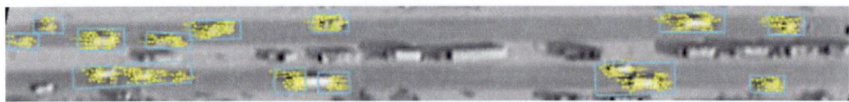

Figure 2.3: Clustering (cyan) of independent motion vectors (yellow) with clearly visible under- and over-segmentation.

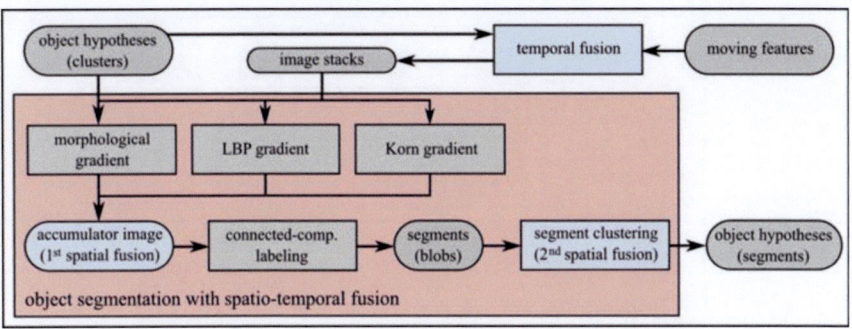

Figure 3.1: The concept of spatio-temporally fused object segmentation.

3.1 Spatio-Temporally Fused Object Segmentation

To handle such problems, more sophisticated segmentation approaches have to be introduced. In order to avoid model assumptions limiting the generality of the approach, the only assumptions made are that objects are rectangular and the motion direction corresponds to the object orientation. Hence, the best fitting bounding box has to be found. For the identification of object pixels, contour extraction algorithms are implemented. Therefore, methods for gradient magnitude calculation in combination with a connected-component labeling algorithm are investigated. Gradients are calculated with a Canny-like algorithm [Kor88], morphological operations [LHS87], and Local Binary Patterns [TB12]. Connected-component labeling is preferred to identify contiguous contour segments as other approaches such as standard watershed segmentation or Graph-Cuts [Bra00] failed due to partially weak contrast.

For higher robustness, methods for spatio-temporal fusion of these approaches are investigated. The concept is shown in Fig. 3.1. Regions of interest are provided by moving local feature clustering (cyan boxes). Temporal fusion of these regions of interest is applied using the tracked moving local features to generate image stacks [TK12b]. In these stacks, image to image registration is focusing on the moving object. Hence, the moving object remains in the same position along the consecutive images in the stack and the background appears to move. By calculating the pixel-wise mean gray-value, the background is more and more blurred and disappears after some time. This is visualized in Fig. 3.2. The original region of interest and the generated mean images of the related stacks are processed with the contour extraction algorithms. For the first spatial fusion, the outputs of all algorithms are written to a common gradient magnitude accumulator image. This

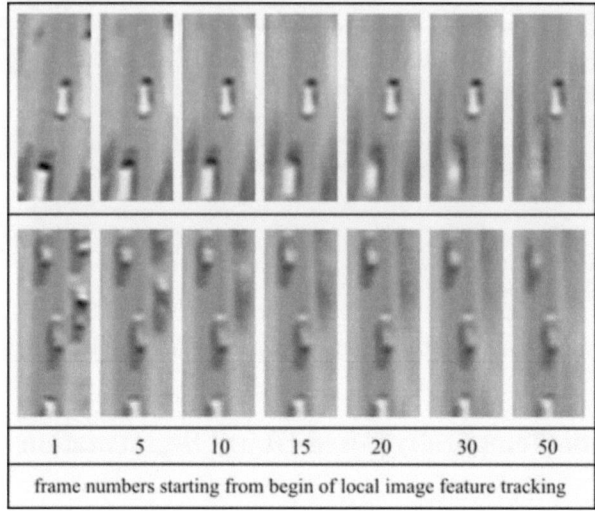

Figure 3.2: Temporal fusion (image stacking) for two local features tracked along 50 frames [TK12b]. The central vehicle is moving and stacked.

provides a more robust result compared to using only one of the algorithms. Object contour pixels are detected by connected-component labeling with adaptive thresholding [TK12b] in the accumulator image. After morphological closing, a bounding box is generated around these object pixels using the shape and orientation assumptions mentioned earlier. Since several regions for the same object are processed, these results have to be clustered in the second spatial fusion. Finally, one segment per object is the output of the object segmentation module.

3.2   Experimental Results

One evaluation scene was manually labeled for the exact number, location, and size of the moving objects. The scene consists of 370 single images with a resolution of 687×547 pixels. 43 different moving objects appear on a busy inner-city street with several overtaking maneuvers. The size of a standard vehicle in the image plane is 15×5 pixels. The segmentation performance was evaluated for completeness and preciseness. Completeness describes the quantity of correct segmentations in percentage and preciseness the quality in mean pixel errors for object position and size. Fig. 3.3 shows the results.

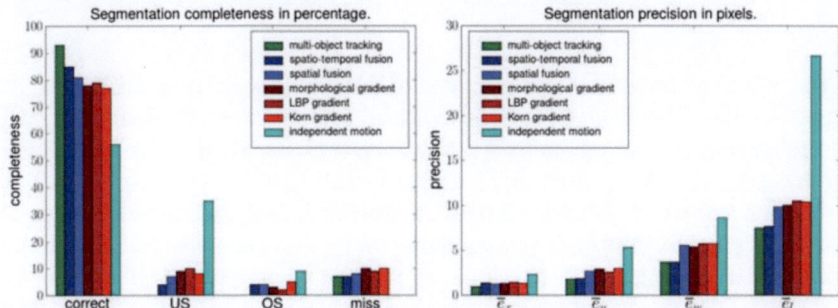

Figure 3.3: Evaluation of completeness (left) and precision (right) of object segmentation using different approaches. Completeness is given in percentage of correct, under-segmented (US), over-segmented (OS), and missed segmentations, precision is given in mean pixel error for object position (x, y) and size (w, l).

Completeness is classified for correct, under-segmentation, over-segmentation, and missed segmentation. Precision is evaluated by the mean errors $\bar{e}_x$ and $\bar{e}_y$ for the object center, and $\bar{e}_w$ and $\bar{e}_l$ for object width and length estimation. Local feature clustering severely suffers from under-segmentation. This causes a weak completeness rate and a high mean error for object length estimation. The single object segmentation approaches significantly improve the results, but none of them clearly outperforms the others. By spatial fusion (without image stacks) of all three algorithms, the performance can be enhanced slightly, while the spatio-temporal fusion shows strong improvement. The benefit of using spatio-temporal segmentation compared to independent motion clustering is visualized in Fig. 3.4. In addition to the described object segmentation approaches, object tracking as proposed in [TK12a] was evaluated and shows the importance of subsequent multi-object tracking after segmentation. Both completeness and preciseness are improved by the introduction of tracking.

Figure 3.4: Spatio-temporal segmentation (red boxes) compared to independent motion clustering (cyan boxes).

4   Classification

The aim of classification in the context of this report is either to distinguish true
positive detections from false positive detections (object recognition) or to assign
verified detections to preliminary defined object classes such as person or vehicle
(object classification). Both problems can be solved with similar methods. From
detected regions of interests, features are extracted, analyzed, and evaluated. The
features providing the highest separability for a given classification task are combined to a descriptor. Finally, with a set of labeled descriptors (training samples),
machine learning algorithms such as k-Nearest-Neighbor (k-NN) classifier, Bayes
classifier, or Support Vector Machine (SVM) are trained. There is a huge variety of concepts and implementations for each of these steps as well as different
combinations.

In this section, however, the focus lies on utilizing the temporal context for these
algorithms. This idea is not new since methods such as Recurrent Neural Networks
(RNN) or Hidden Markov Models (HMM) are well-known and established for
modeling and recognizing temporal patterns for activities, behaviors or situations.
Different states and transitions between states are defined to set up those models.
In contrast, no temporal patterns are to be recognized in this report, but temporal
context shall be used to achieve higher robustness and reliability for the mentioned
machine learning algorithms. Object state, perspective, or appearance will not
change or vary significantly during the observation, but even the consideration
and suppression of noise effects along several consecutive images for example can
increase the classification performance.

4.1   Concepts for Temporally Fused Object Classification

The main idea is to apply a temporal information fusion to support object classification. This fusion can take place on data, feature, or decision level. It is assumed,
that detection, segmentation, and tracking were successfully performed and image
stacks such as the ones in Fig. 3.2 are available for the temporal fusion.

4.1.1   Temporal Fusion on Data Level

For fusion on data level, only the incoming detected and tracked regions of interest
are considered but no further processing such as feature extraction. With image
stacking, not only the background can be blurred as in Section 3, but also noise
can be suppressed by calculating pixel-wise mean or median along few images.

Since the objects observed in this report are of very small size in the image plane due to the high distance, the resolution is rather low. Super-resolution [FREM04] is an approach using image stacks of moving objects or stationary objects in case of a moving camera to artificially enhance the resolution for an image region. After successful registration of several images where the object is not severely changing its appearance, each object pixel offers redundant information. A new pixel grid of higher resolution is created and the pixel values are interpolated using this redundant information. The resulting images are of higher quality due to noise suppression and are more detailed due to the enhanced resolution [HEKS10].

4.1.2 Temporal Fusion on Feature Level

Fusion on feature level is either the feature-wise fusion along several images to create a temporal feature, or the combination of several features along several images to create a descriptor containing temporal information for the subsequent classifier.

An easy way of introducing temporal information to a feature is calculating its mean or median value for several consecutive time steps. If the mean pixel value in a region of interest is, for example, used as feature for example and its value is affected by noise in the current time step, then calculating its median value considering the last time steps will improve the classification result. More sophisticated temporal features are Histograms of Spatiotemporal Gradients (STHOG) [RCPH12] or Local Binary Pattern (LBP) histograms from three orthogonal planes (LBP-TOP) [ZAMP12]. These features typically work best with a short temporal context of ten or less time steps [RCPH12].

The combination of several features is usually done by concatenating the descriptors of several time steps. This way, a new descriptor of much higher dimensionality is generated containing the temporal information. To avoid the curse of dimensionality, this fusion has also to be done in short temporal context. With this temporal descriptor, standard classifiers such as k-NN or SVM can be trained and are expected to achieve more robust results than without temporal context. In addition to the high dimensionality of the descriptor, one big drawback is the fixed size of the descriptor which is mandatory for the application of most parametric classifiers such as SVM. A more flexible way of feature fusion is possible for the Naïve Bayes classifier. Therefore, the features have to be conditionally independent. This can be achieved by using Principal Component Analysis (PCA), which results in pairwise independent features, or by applying Independent Component Analysis (ICA). It is assumed that each feature has its own probability distribution model. For the current time step the likelihood of each feature can be calculated. When using Naïve Bayes, the posterior probability that a sample belonging to a specific class is then given by the product of the prior probability and all likelihoods. This also means that not all features have to be considered: if a feature is of bad quality, its likelihood can be excluded from the product, which is an easy way for on-line adaptation of the descriptor. Furthermore, there are posterior probabilities for each class available after each time step.

4.1.3 Temporal Fusion on Decision Level

For fusion on decision level, not only the classification result of the current time step but also the results of several time steps in the past are considered to make a temporally more stable decision. If a SVM in the current time step decides for class A but decided for class A in two and class B in four out of the last six time steps, a simple voting approach would decide for class B in the current time step, too, as the voting result would be 4:3. The main advantage of this method is that considering a longer history will not affect the runtime in comparison to feature level fusion. Furthermore, the curse of dimensionality is not a problem as well.

This kind of fusion can be applied easily for all kind of classifiers. The combination of several fusion approaches coming from different fusion levels is possible, too, and could be a way to combine short term history as used on feature level and long term history on decision level. However, such concepts are still to be implemented and evaluated.

5 Conclusion

Utilizing temporal information for video surveillance is a very promising approach. It is well-known from multi-object tracking that problems appearing in single images such as occlusions or split and merged object detections can be solved well with appropriate tracking algorithms and strategies. This idea can be used for other machine vision tasks, too, such as object detection and segmentation. Several methods were presented and discussed in this report with a focus on remote surveillance. Some experiments using real UAV surveillance data showed convincing results. Furthermore, concepts were presented for object recognition and classification with temporal context. Future work will include the implementation and evaluation of these methods using the UAV data.

Bibliography

[Bra00]   G. Bradski. The OpenCV Library. *Dr. Dobb's Journal of Software Tools*, 2000.

[CLYL11]   Xianbin Cao, Jinhe Lan, Pingkun Yan, and Xuelong Li. KLT Feature Based Vehicle
           Detection and Tracking in Airborne Videos. In *Proc. of the Intern. Conf. on Image and
           Graphics*, Hefei, China, 2011.

[DT05]   Navneet Dalal and Bill Triggs. Histograms of Oriented Gradients for Human Detection.
           In *Proceedings of the IEEE International Conference on Computer Vision and Pattern
           Recognition (CVPR)*, pages 886–893, San Diego, CA, USA, June 2005.

[FREM04]   Sina Farsiu, M. Dirk Robinson, Michael Elad, and Peyman Milanfar. Fast and Robust
           Multiframe Super Resolution. *IEEE Transactions on Image Processing*, 13(10):1327–
           1344, October 2004.

[HEKS08]   Norbert Heinze, Martin Esswein, Wolfgang Krüger, and Günter Saur. Automatic im-
           age exploitation system for small UAVs. In *Proc. of SPIE Vol. 6946, Airborne intel-
           ligence, surveillance, reconnaissance (ISR) systems and applications V*, Orlando, FL,
           USA, March 2008.

[HEKS10]   Norbert Heinze, Martin Esswein, Wolfgang Krüger, and Günter Saur. Image exploitation
           algorithms for reconnaissance and surveillance with UAV. In *Proceedings of SPIE Vol.
           7668, Airborne intelligence, surveillance, reconnaissance (ISR) systems and applications
           VII*, Orlando, FL, USA, April 2010.

[HSD73]   Robert M. Haralick, K. Shanmugam, and Its'hak Dinstein. Textural Features for Im-
           age Classification. *IEEE Transactions on Systems, Man and Cybernetics*, 3(6):610–621,
           November 1973.

[IA98]   M. Irani and P. Anandan. A unified approach to moving object detection in 2D and 3D
           scenes. *IEEE Transactions on Pattern Analysis and Machine Intelligence*, 20(6):577–
           589, June 1998.

[ICS+10]   Aryo Wiman Nur Ibrahim, Pang Wee Ching, Gerald Seet, Michael Lau, and Witold Cza-
           jewski. Moving Objects Detection and Tracking Framework for UAV-based Surveillance.
           In *Proceedings of the Fourth Pacific-Rim Symposium on Image and Video Technology*,
           Singapore, November 2010.

[IKN98]   Laurent Itti, Christof Koch, and Ernst Niebur. A Model of Saliency-Based Visual At-
           tention for Rapid Scene Analysis. *IEEE Transactions on Pattern Analysis and Machine
           Intelligence*, 20(11):1254–1259, November 1998.

[JA11]   Kai Jüngling and Michael Arens. Hierarchical object detection and tracking with an Im-
           plicit Shape Model. In *International Conference on Image Processing, Computer Vision,
           and Pattern Recognition (IPCV)*, Las Vegas, NV, USA, July 2011.

[Kor88]   Axel Korn. Toward a Symbolic Representation of Intensity Changes in Images. *IEEE
           Transactions on Pattern Analysis and Machine Intelligence*, 10(5):610–625, September
           1988.

[KSS+01]   R. Kumar, H. Sawhney, S. Samarasekera, S. Hsu, Hai Tao, Yanlin Guo, K. Hanna,
           A. Pope, R. Wildes, D. Hirvonen, M. Hansen, and P. Burt. Aerial video surveillance
           and exploitation. *Proc. of the IEEE*, 89(10):1518–1539, October 2001.

[LHS87]   James S. J. Lee, Robert M. Haralick, and Linda G. Shapiro. Morphologic edge detection.
           IEEE Journal of Robotics and Automation, 3(2):142–156, April 1987.

[Low04]   David G. Lowe. Distinctive Image Features from Scale-Invariant Keypoints. *Intern. Journal of Computer Vision*, 60(2):91–110, 2004.

[MCUP02]   Jiri Matas, Ondrej Chum, Martin Urban, and Tomas Pajdla. Robust wide baseline stereo from maximally stable extremal regions. In *Proceedings of the British Machine Vision Conference (BMVC)*, Cardiff, UK, September 2002.

[PSH$^+$06] A. G. Amitha Perera, Chukka Srinivas, Anthony Hoogs, Glen Brooksby, and Wensheng Hu. Multi-Object Tracking Through Simultaneous Long Occlusions and Split-Merge Conditions. In *Proc. of the IEEE CVPR*, New York, NY, USA, 2006.

[RCPH12]   Kishore K. Reddy, Naresh Cuntoor, Amitha Perera, and Anthony Hoogs. Human Action Recognition in Large-Scale Datasets Using Histogram of Spatiotemporal Gradients. In *Proceedings of the IEEE International Conference on Advanced Video and Signal-Based Surveillance (AVSS)*, Beijing, China, September 2012.

[RIS10]   Vladimir Reilly, Haroon Idrees, and Mubarak Shah. Detection and Tracking of Large Number of Targets in Wide Area Surveillance. In *Proceedings of the 11th European Conference on Computer Vision (ECCV)*, Heraklion, Greece, September 2010.

[ST94]   Jianbo Shi and C. Tomasi. Good features to track. In *Proceedings of the 1994 IEEE Computer Society Conference on Computer Vision and Pattern Recognition (CVPR)*, pages 593–600, Seattle, WA, USA, June 1994.

[TB12]   Michael Teutsch and Jürgen Beyerer. Noise Resistant Gradient Calculation and Edge Detection using Local Binary Patterns. In *Proceedings of the International Workshop on Computer Vision with Local Binary Pattern Variants (LBP) in Conjunction with the Asian Conference on Computer Vision (ACCV)*, Daejeon, Korea, November 2012.

[TK12a]   Michael Teutsch and Wolfgang Krüger. Detection, Segmentation, and Tracking of Moving Objects in UAV Videos. In *Proceedings of the IEEE International Conference on Advanced Video and Signal-Based Surveillance (AVSS)*, Beijing, China, September 2012.

[TK12b]   Michael Teutsch and Wolfgang Krüger. Spatio-Temporal Fusion of Object Segmentation Approaches for Moving Distant Targets. In *Proceedings of the International Conference on Information Fusion (FUSION)*, Singapore, July 2012.

[VJ01]   Paul Viola and Michael Jones. Robust Real-time Object Detection. *International Journal of Computer Vision*, 2001.

[XCSH10]   Jiangjian Xiao, Hui Cheng, Harpreet Sawhney, and Feng Han. Vehicle Detection and Tracking in Wide Field-of-View Aerial Video. In *Proc. of the IEEE Conference on Computer Vision and Pattern Recognition (CVPR)*, San Francisco, CA, USA, 2010.

[YMKC07]   Chang Yuan, G. Medioni, Jinman Kang, and I. Cohen. Detecting motion regions in the presence of a strong parallax from a moving camera by multiview geometric constraints. *IEEE Transactions on Pattern Analysis and Machine Intelligence*, 29(9):1627–1641, September 2007.

[YSM08]   Fenghui Yao, Ali Sekmen, and Mohan J. Malkani. Multiple moving target detection, tracking, and recognition from a moving observer. In *Proc. of the IEEE Intern. Conf. on Information and Automation (ICIA)*, Hunan, China, June 2008.

[ZAMP12]   Guoying Zhao, Timo Ahonen, Jiri Matas, and Matti Pietikäinen. Rotation-Invariant Image and Video Description With Local Binary Pattern Features. *IEEE Transactions on Image Processing*, 21(4):1465–1477, April 2012.

[Zha05]   Shuqun Zhang. Object Tracking in Unmanned Aerial Vehicle (UAV) Videos Using a Combined Approach. In *Proceedings of the IEEE International Conference on Acoustics, Speech, and Signal Processing (ICASSP)*, Philadelphia, PA, USA, March 2005.

Probabilistic Greedy Planning of Deflectometric Measurements

Masoud Roschani

Vision and Fusion Lab
Institute for Anthropomatics
Karlsruhe Institute of Technology (KIT), Germany
masoud.roschani@kit.edu

Technical Report IES-2012-04

Abstract:

During a deflectometric inspection, the size of an object or the complexity of its shape may prevent one from capturing the whole surface with a single measurement or with uniform resolution. Selecting sensor configurations manually is a tedious task and not trivial for complex shaped surfaces. We introduce a greedy planning procedure which iteratively finds the next best sensor configuration with respect to an optimality criterion based on uncertainty. We show possibilities to decrease the runtime by considering the locality of the measurement and the sparse representation of the surface.

1   Introduction

Visibility is a general problem of visual inspection tasks. Especially in deflectometry, where the test object is part of the measurement mapping and can only be observed indirectly. Depending on the size of the pattern generator only small regions of the test object may be observed. E.g. the viewing area on convex shaped objects decreases with increasing convex curvature because the light rays, when observed from the camera, expand. Therefore a set of measurements has to be made and subsequently fused together. The difficulty here is to select appropriate sensor configurations (i.e. position and orientation of the display and camera) for the deflectometric sensor. Manually choosing sensor configurations is not trivial and for complex shaped objects it is a time consuming task.

We investigate an automatic determination of sensor configurations for the deflectometric inspection task. I.e. we assume that a reference surface is given (e.g. in

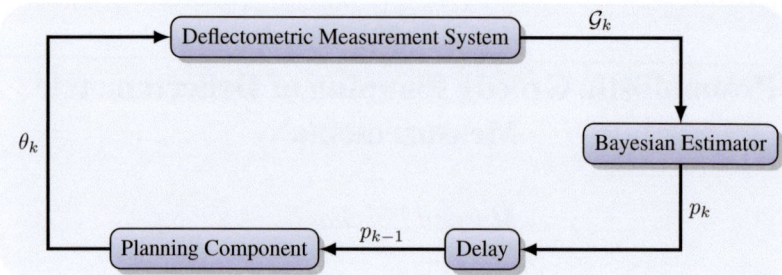

Figure 1.1: Planning takes place in a loop. At time step k a sensor configuration θ_k is chosen based on the current estimation of the surface. This leads to a new measurement, which in turn is used to update the estimation p_k.

form of a CAD model) and the test object has only small deviations from it. Then, we choose a sequence of sensor configurations, also called a *plan*, which covers the whole surface with high accuracy.

The planning procedure is executed in a loop, see Fig. 1.1. In every time step a local measurement is made and used to update the current estimation of the surface. We choose a probabilistic representation of the surface because it allows fusing new measurements using Bayesian inference and the consideration of measurement noise. The updated estimation is used by the planning component as a basis for choosing the next sensor configuration. For that, an optimization problem is solved with a criteria of maximizing the information gain of the next measurement. An optimal planning algorithm would consider the whole planning horizon. However, due to its complexity, we consider only the information gain of the next measurement. For this reason the introduced planning procedure is called *greedy*. In literature this is also called *next best view planning*, see for instance [WDAN07],[DBF09] or [DF09].

The remaining part of the report is divided as follows. In section 2 we briefly review the deflectometric measurement process and formulate the problem of surface reconstruction from deflectometric measurements with a given reference surface as a regression problem. In section 3 we present the surface representation and a Bayesian regression model for estimating the surface. The planning procedure is described in section 4 and an accelerated version in section 5. Finally in section 6 we show the acceleration rate of the fast algorithm compared to the naive algorithm in a simulation test case. We conclude with a discussion in section 7.

2   Measurement model

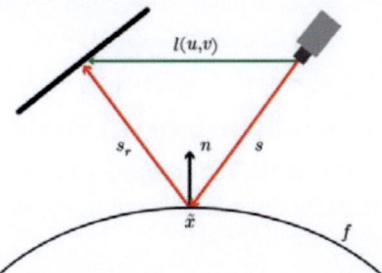

Figure 2.1: This figure shows the inverted deflectometric light path of a ray from the camera pixel (u, v) to the display (red arrows). A deflectometric measurement provides a mapping $l(u, v)$ from camera pixel to display points (green arrow).

In this section we briefly introduce the deflectometric measurement model. For a more detailed description we refer to [Wer11]. We assume that a reference surface is given (e.g. in form of a CAD model) and the test surface differs slightly from it.

A typical deflectometric setup consists of a specular test object, a camera and an LCD. The LCD shows a sequence of patterns which encodes every single pixel. Due to the nonlinear shape of the test object the camera observes deformed images of the pattern. Through a decoding process (e.g. phase-shift method) a mapping between camera pixel and LCD pixel can be established. It can further be used to deduce measured gradients of the surface.

Fig. 2.1 shows a ray path from a camera pixel reflected on the test surface towards the LCD. If the measurement model is calibrated (i.e. position and orientation of the camera and LCD as well as the intrinsic parameters of the camera are known) the direction of the vector s is known. After a measurement the mapping from camera pixel to LCD pixel in form of the vector l can be determined through the decoding process. The vector s_r of the outgoing ray can be calculated from the mapping vector l and the vector s. For the measured normal we get the relation

$$\hat{n} = \frac{\hat{s}_r - \hat{s}}{\|\hat{s}_r - \hat{s}\|} \qquad \text{with} \qquad \hat{s}_r = \frac{l - s}{\|l - s\|}, \qquad (2.1)$$

where a hat over a vector x means that it is normalized $\hat{x} = \frac{x}{\|x\|}$. Because the length of s is generally unknown (the intersection point $\tilde{x}$ with the surface is unknown) only a set of possible normals along the ray can be determined [Bal08]. However, assuming that a reference surface is given, we can use it to approximate the length of s. This solely works when the measured surface deviates only slightly from the reference surface.

Finally we get the gradient of the intersection point $\tilde{x}$ with

$$g_{\tilde{x}} = \begin{pmatrix} \hat{n}_1/\hat{n}_3 \\ \hat{n}_2/\hat{n}_3 \end{pmatrix},$$

where $\hat{n}_1, \hat{n}_2, \hat{n}_3$ are the components of the normal in Equation (2.1).

Thus, we can formulate the problem of estimating the surface height as a regression problem. Each measurement provides a set of gradients of specific points of the surface which serve as the training data.

3 Probabilistic Surface Representation and Inference

We consider a probabilistic planning approach, therefore we need an estimation procedure which is able to specify an uncertainty of the estimate. In [RB12] we formulated the problem as a Gaussian Process Regression problem and then approximated the Gaussian Process with a parametric model. Here we will derive the model directly by assuming a parametric model from the beginning.

Before we begin with the derivation of the inference method we have to introduce some notation. Let $X = (x_1, \ldots, x_m)$ be a sequence of elements and $\phi(x)$ an arbitrary function. Then we define $\phi(X) := (\phi(x_1), \ldots, \phi(x_m))^T$ as the column vector which results by applying ϕ to every element of x and stacking the results together. This definition contains also the following cases: If $\phi(x) \in \mathbb{R}^d$ is a column vector, then $\phi(X) \in \mathbb{R}^{m \cdot d}$ is a column vector. If $\phi(x) \in \mathbb{R}^{1 \times d}$ is a row vector, then $\phi(X) \in \mathbb{R}^{m \times d}$ is a matrix.

We use a standard Bayesian Linear Regression model and express the surface as a function of the form

$$f(x) = \sum_{i=1}^{m} \alpha_i \phi_i(x), \tag{3.1}$$

where $\phi_i(x)$ are appropriate basis functions weighted by α_i. With the definitions $\Phi(x) = (\phi_1(x), \ldots, \phi_m(x))$ and $\alpha = (\alpha_i, \ldots, \alpha_m)^T$ we can also write (3.1) in matrix-vector form as $f(x) = \Phi(x)\alpha$. The weights are modeled as a random variables and have a prior distribution

$$\alpha \sim \mathcal{N}(\mu_\alpha, \Sigma_\alpha).$$

Note that we will sometimes refer to the function f itself as a surface and to $f(x)$ for arbitrary x as function values or surface height values, interchangeably.

Let the training data $\mathcal{D} = (\mathcal{X}, \mathcal{Q})$ be given which consists of measured gradient values $\mathcal{Q} = (q_1, \ldots, q_n)$ and corresponding positions $\mathcal{X} = (x_1, \ldots, x_n)$. The measured gradients are assumed to be the surface gradients superimposed with additive noise:

$$q_i = \nabla f(x_i) + \rho_i.$$

The observation noises $\rho_i \sim \mathcal{N}(0, \Sigma_{\rho_i})$ are considered to be Gaussian and independent. The joint distribution of the noise $\rho := (\rho_1, \ldots, \rho_n)^T$ is Gaussian with zero mean and a covariance matrix with block diagonal elements equal to Σ_{ρ_i}. We will denote this covariance matrix with Σ_N.

For what follows we introduce the notation $\mathbf{f}^\star := f(\mathcal{X}^\star)$ and $\mathbf{g}_{\mathcal{X}} := \nabla f(\mathcal{X}) + \rho$. We aim to calculate the predictive distribution $p(\mathbf{f}^\star \mid \mathcal{X}^\star, \mathcal{D})$ of unknown values $\mathbf{f}^\star$ on positions $\mathcal{X}^\star$. This gives us a distribution over a discretized surface.

The joint distribution of $\mathbf{g}_{\mathcal{X}}$ and $\mathbf{f}^\star$ is a Gaussian distribution

$$\begin{pmatrix} \mathbf{f}^\star \\ \mathbf{g}_{\mathcal{X}} \end{pmatrix} \sim \mathcal{N}\left(\begin{pmatrix} \Phi(\mathcal{X}^\star)\mu_\alpha \\ \nabla\Phi(\mathcal{X}^\star)\mu_\alpha \end{pmatrix}, \begin{pmatrix} K_{11} & K_{12} \\ K_{12}^T & K_{22} \end{pmatrix} \right),$$

where the individual elements of the covariance matrix are block matrices and derived as follows:

$$\begin{aligned} K_{11} &= \mathrm{Cov}\left\{ \mathbf{f}^\star, \mathbf{f}^\star \right\} \\ &= \mathrm{Cov}\left\{ \Phi(\mathcal{X}^\star)\alpha, \Phi(\mathcal{X}^\star)\alpha \right\} \\ &= \Phi(\mathcal{X}^\star)\Sigma_\alpha\Phi(\mathcal{X}^\star)^T \end{aligned}$$

$$\begin{aligned} K_{22} &= \mathrm{Cov}\left\{ \mathbf{g}_{\mathcal{X}}, \mathbf{g}_{\mathcal{X}} \right\} \\ &= \mathrm{Cov}\left\{ \nabla\Phi(\mathcal{X})\alpha + \rho, \nabla\Phi(\mathcal{X})\alpha + \rho \right\} \\ &= \nabla\Phi(\mathcal{X})\Sigma_\alpha\nabla\Phi(\mathcal{X})^T + \mathrm{Cov}\left\{ \rho, \rho \right\} + 2\underbrace{\mathrm{Cov}\left\{ \nabla\Phi(\mathcal{X})\alpha, \rho \right\}}_{=0} \\ &= \Phi(\mathcal{X})\Sigma_\alpha\Phi(\mathcal{X})^T + \Sigma_N \end{aligned}$$

$$\begin{aligned} K_{12} &= \mathrm{Cov}\left\{ \mathbf{f}^\star, \mathbf{g}_{\mathcal{X}} \right\} \\ &= \mathrm{Cov}\left\{ \Phi(\mathcal{X}^\star)\alpha, \nabla\Phi(\mathcal{X})\alpha + \rho \right\} \\ &= \Phi(\mathcal{X}^\star)\Sigma_\alpha\nabla\Phi(\mathcal{X})^T + \underbrace{\mathrm{Cov}\left\{ \Phi(\mathcal{X}^\star)\alpha, \rho \right\}}_{=0} \end{aligned}$$

$$= \Phi(\mathcal{X}^\star)\Sigma_\alpha \nabla\Phi(\mathcal{X})^T.$$

The marked terms in the derivation above are zero because it is assumed that the noise ρ is independent of the weights α. The predictive distribution is obtained by dividing the joint distribution with $p(\mathbf{g}_\mathcal{X} = \mathcal{Q})$. This is a standard Gaussian operation and we get the following expressions for the expectation and covariance matrix of $p\left(\mathbf{f}^\star \mid \mathcal{X}^\star, \mathcal{D}\right)$:

$$\mu^\star = \Phi(\mathcal{X}^\star)\mu_\alpha + K_{12}K_{22}^{-1}(\mathcal{Q} - \nabla\Phi(\mathcal{X}^\star)\mu_\alpha)$$
$$\Sigma^\star = K_{11} - K_{12}K_{22}^{-1}K_{12}^T.$$

4 Planning

In the previous section it was shown how to estimate a surface given a set of measurements. Now we consider the automatic selection of sensor configurations.

We want to find a sequence of sensor configurations which is optimal in the following sense. First we define a reward function which measures the goodness of one measurement. The goodness of a plan is then measured as the sum of all rewards obtained from all its measurements. Because this optimization is very sophisticated, we approximate it by only considering the first term, i.e. we make a greedy approximation. This leads to a recursive computation of the plan. At time step k sensor configurations $\theta_{1:k}$ are already planned and their corresponding measurements $\mathcal{D}_{1:k}$ are fused together to yield the predictive distribution $p_k(\mathbf{f}^\star) := p\left(\mathbf{f}^\star \mid \mathcal{D}_{1:k}\right)$. This distribution summarizes approximately all information about the measurements. The next sensor configuration is obtained by solving a greedy optimization problem

$$\theta_{k+1} = \underset{\theta \in \Omega}{\arg\max}\, g(p_k, \theta), \tag{4.1}$$

where g is the reward function. This optimization may still be hard to compute, because it might have too many local maxima depending on the current estimation probability p_k.

In the first subsection we define the reward function. Its evaluation may take too long depending on the inference method and the number of pixels on the camera. Therefore we also discuss possible approximation methods.

In the second subsection we study the parameter space Ω. We choose a parametrization which considers the reference surface and allows obtaining good starting values. Furthermore this parametrization also allows a partial discretization of the sensor configuration space which assures not to get stuck in local maxima.

4.1   Reward Function

One way to obtain the goodness of a sensor configuration θ given an estimation p_k of the surface, we have to first simulate the corresponding deflectometric measurement (this yields gradient data) and than update the estimation to yield a hypothetical next estimation $\tilde{p}_{k+1}$. The variance of this distribution compared with the variance of the current estimation p_k is defined as the reward

$$g(p_k, \theta) = \text{Var}\left\{p_k\right\} - \text{Var}\left\{\tilde{p}_{k+1}\right\}$$

and is also called the information gain. This value is always positive because intuitively measurements lead to information which always reduce the variance. This is also known as the "information never hurts" principle. Generally it is possible to use other uncertainty criteria than the variance like the entropy of p_k, see for example [WDAN07]. The complexity of a single evaluation of the cost function depends on the number of camera pixels and evaluation points $\mathcal{X}^\star$. The evaluation points should be chosen in such a way that the surface is adequately covered. An approximation of the reward function may be obtained by approximating the deflectometric simulation. Only a small amount of rays could be traced. This reduces the simulation and also the inference effort because less data is given for the inference step.

4.2   Sensor Configuration Space

The sensor configuration of a deflectometric sensor system consists of the position and orientation of the camera and the display. Further possible parameters are intrinsic camera parameters like focal length and aperture. But we will not consider them here and assume them to be fixed. With a given reference surface the following parametrization of the sensor configuration can be chosen (see also Fig. 4.1 for an illustration):

- The first parameter is a focus point x_0, lying on the reference surface. This point serves a twofold purpose. First we pose the constraint that the optical axis of the camera intersects this point. Thereby we ensure that the camera will at least observe one point on the surface. Second we define a frame

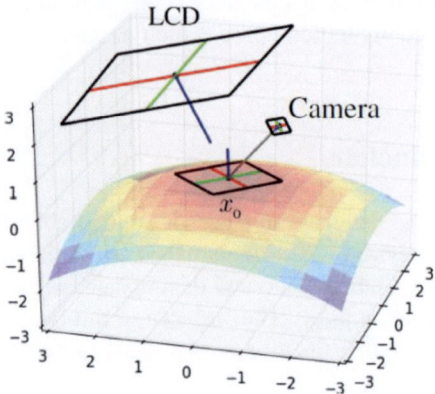

Figure 4.1: This figure depicts the sensor configuration, i.e. the focus point x_0 with the attached frame and the camera as well as the LCD.

on the focus point which characterizes the intrinsic properties of the reference surface. The remaining parameters will be parametrized relative to the frame. This allows an invariant positioning of the sensor regarding translation and rotation of the surface. The frame is chosen such that its x-axis is the normalized gradient, the z-axis is the normalized normal of the surface at the focus point and the y-axis is chosen such that it is orthogonal to the other axis.

- The camera is parametrized by its elevation and azimuth angle and the distance to the surface regarding the focus point. The remaining free parameter is a rotation about the optical axis of the camera.

- The position of the display is parametrized by spherical coordinates and its orientation in Euler coordinates. Compared to the camera the display is not constrained. This is necessary to ensure that the displayed pattern can always be captured by the camera.

We will often split the sensor configuration into two parts, i.e. the focus point component x and the remaining parameters $\tilde{\theta}_x \in \tilde{\Omega}$ and write $\theta = (x, \tilde{\theta}_x)$.

We propose a partial discretization of the sensor configuration space by choosing the focus point component only from a finite set of points on the surface, see Fig. 4.2 for an illustration. The optimization in Eq.(4.1) can be reformulated and solved as a two-layered hierarchical algorithm. In every time step the lower layer determines the optimal remaining sensor configurations $\tilde{\theta}_x^\star$ for all focus points by

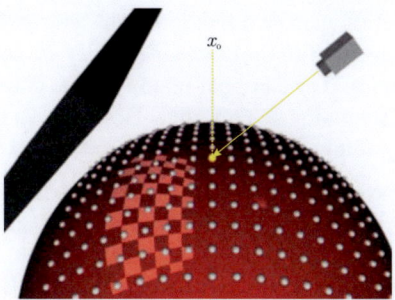

Figure 4.2: The sensor configuration set Ω is partially discretized by choosing the focus point component from a finite set. The figure depicts the focus points as balls distributed on a grid.

solving $\tilde{\theta}_x^\star = \arg\max_{\tilde{\theta}\in\tilde{\Omega}} g(p_k, (x, \tilde{\theta}))$. (Note that $\tilde{\theta}_x^\star$ depends also on the time step which is dropped here for clarity.) It also yields the optimal information gain that can be obtained on every focus point for that particular time step. Based on the solution of the lower layer the higher layer chooses the sensor configuration with the largest information gain. This procedure is depicted in Algorithm 4.1.

Algorithm 4.1 Naive Greedy Optimization

---
for all time steps $k = 0 \dots T$ **do**

    for all focus points $\{x_i, i = 1 \dots N\}$ **do**

        $g_i, \tilde{\theta}_i^\star \leftarrow \max_{\tilde{\theta}} g(p_i, (x_i, \tilde{\theta}))$

    end for

    $\theta_{k+1} \leftarrow (x_i, \tilde{\theta}_i^\star)$ with maximal g_i

    $p_{k+1} \leftarrow$ forward simulation and inference with θ_{k+1}

end for

---

5 Speeding up greedy planning

Algorithm 4.1 recalculates the information gain for the focus points in every time step. This can be very time consuming if the surface is very large. There are two properties which make it possible to speed up the planning process. The first one is the already mentioned "information never hurts" principle which, in our case, more formally states that we have the following inequality

$$g(p_k, \theta) \geq g(p_{k+1}, \theta), \quad \forall \theta \in \Omega. \tag{5.1}$$

In words, the information gain of a measurement with any sensor configuration θ decreases as time goes by. With the above inequality we could use the information gain from the last time step as an upper bound for the current time step. But only, when the sensor configuration is constant. However, in our case, we might get another sensor configuration for the same focus point x at every time step.

The other important property is the fact that for every focus point x we choose the remaining configuration so that the information gain is maximal, i.e. we have

$$g(p_k, (x, \tilde{\theta}_k^\star)) \geq g(p_k, (x, \tilde{\theta})), \quad \forall \tilde{\theta} \in \tilde{\Omega}, \tag{5.2}$$

where $\tilde{\theta}_k^\star$ is the optimal configuration chosen for focus point x at time step k. Together we can deduce

$$g(p_k, (x, \tilde{\theta}_k^\star)) \geq g(p_k, (x, \tilde{\theta}_{k+1}^\star)) \geq g(p_{k+1}, (x, \tilde{\theta}_{k+1}^\star)). \tag{5.3}$$

The first inequality is due to (5.2) and the second inequality due to (5.1). Inequality (5.3) states that the information gain calculated for the focus point x on time step k can be used as an upper bound for the successive information gains on x (although the sensor configuration parameter for a focus point may change at every time step).

This insight can be used in an optimization algorithm, depicted in Algorithms 5.1 and 5.2. In a first step all information gain values for all points are computed (Initialization). The algorithm maintains the information gain values as a priority queue. We differentiate between two types of values: upper bounds, taken from the previous steps or exact values, calculated with $g(p, \theta)$. In every time step we choose the sensor configuration with the highest value from the queue. If it is an upper bound we calculate the real value and put it back in the queue. We repeat this process until a sensor configuration with a correct value is chosen. This sensor configuration is selected. Afterwards a new information gain is calculated and the new sensor configuration is put back to the queue.

Algorithm 5.1 Initialization

$L \leftarrow [\,]$
for all focus points $\{x_i, i = 1 \dots N\}$ **do**
$\quad g_i, \tilde{\theta}_i^\star \leftarrow \max_{\tilde{\theta}} g(p_k, (x_i, \tilde{\theta}))$
$\quad L \leftarrow (g_i, (x_i, \tilde{\theta}^\star))$
end for

Algorithm 5.2 Plan Generation

---

for all time steps $k = 0 \ldots T$ **do**
    $(g, (x, \tilde{\theta}^{\star})) \leftarrow$ element with maximal information gain from L
    while g is upper bound **do**
        $g, \tilde{\theta}^{\star} \leftarrow \max_{\tilde{\theta}} g(p_k, (x, \tilde{\theta}))$
        Insert $(g, (x, \tilde{\theta}^{\star}))$ into L
    end while
    $\theta_{k+1} \leftarrow (x, \tilde{\theta}^{\star})$
    Insert $(g, (x, \tilde{\theta}^{\star}))$ into L
    $p_{k+1} \leftarrow$ forward simulation and inference with θ_{k+1}
end for

---

6 Experiments

We compared the naive optimization method to the optimization method with bounds in a simulation test case. The test object is a $600\,mm \times 600\,mm$ region extracted from a sphere with radius $1400\,mm$. The camera is modeled as a pinhole camera with 640×480 pixel. The resolution of the display is 1920×1080 pixel. The focus point component of the sensor configuration is discretized to 16 values, which are spaced evenly on a 4×4 grid. The total number of planning steps is 16. Fig. 6.1 shows the resulting statistics of the planning procedure. Fig. 6.1(a) depicts the number of optimizations plotted against the focus points. It can be seen that the number of optimizations ranges from minimally 2 to maximally 5. A histogram of the number of optimizations is given in Fig. 6.1(b). For comparison, the naive method optimizes all focus points in every planning step. Therefore it executes 16 optimization per focus point during the whole planning procedure. The total complexity reduction is up to 3 to 4 times.

7 Discussion

Summarizing, we have shown a greedy planning algorithm which automatically determines sensor configurations for the next measurement. For this purpose the information gain, measured as the variance reduction, of the next measurement is used. We have shown that the information gain calculated for a focus point x on the surface can be used as an upper bound for the information gain of future measurements. This can be used to speed up the optimization up to 3 to 4 times. The greedy algorithm provides a fast broad covering of the surface but does not

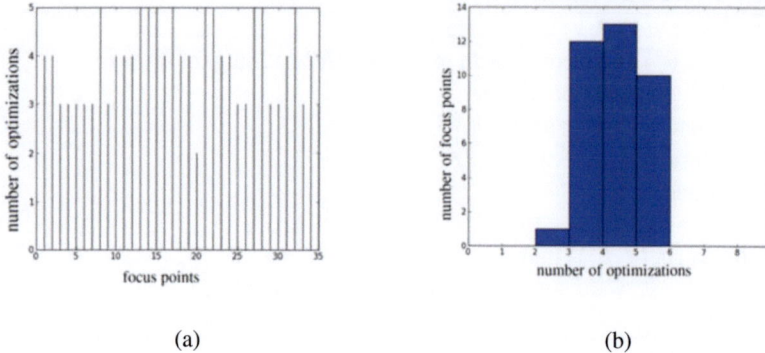

(a)   (b)

Figure 6.1: This figure shows the result statistics of the number of optimizations executed on the focus points during planning. ((a)) shows the number
of optimizations plotted against the focus points, ((b)) shows the corresponding
histogram.

incorporate future measurements. Considering them could improve the total number of measurements needed to measure the surface. This should be investigated
in future work.

Bibliography

[Bal08]   Jonathan Balzer. *Regularisierung des Deflektometrieproblems - Grundlagen und Anwen-
             dung*. PhD thesis, 2008.

[DBF09]   Enrique Dunn, Jur van den Berg, and Jan-Michael Frahm. Developing visual sensing
             strategies through next best view planning. In *Proceedings of the 2009 IEEE/RSJ in-
             ternational conference on Intelligent robots and systems*, IROS'09, pages 4001–4008,
             Piscataway, NJ, USA, 2009. IEEE Press.

[DF09]   Enrique Dunn and Jan-Michael Frahm. Next best view planning for active model
             improvement. In *BMVC*, 2009.

[RB12]   Masoud Roschani and Jürgen Beyerer. Planungsbasierte Oberflächeninspektion in der
             Deflektometrie bei gegebener Referenzfläche mittels Greedy-Optimierung. In Prof.
             Dr.-Ing. Robert Schmitt, editor, *Tagungsband des XXVI. Messtechnisches Symposiums*,
             Aachen, September 2012. Shaker.

[WDAN07]   Stefan Wenhardt, Benjamin Deutsch, Elli Angelopoulou, and Heinrich Niemann. Active
             visual object reconstruction using d-, e-, and t-optimal next best views. *Computer Vision
             and Pattern Recognition, IEEE Computer Society Conference on*, 0:1–7, 2007.

[Wer11]   Stefan Bruno Werling. *Deflektometrie zur automatischen Sichtprüfung und Rekonstruk-
             tion spiegelnder Oberfächen*. PhD thesis, 2011.

Underwater Imaging Model

Thomas Stephan

Vision and Fusion Laboratory
Institute for Anthropomatics
Karlsruhe Institute of Technology (KIT), Germany
thomas.stephan@kit.edu

Technical Report IES-2012-05

Abstract:

Optical imaging under water represents an unresolved problem until to-
day. Poor visibility, blurred images and a minor signal-to-noise-ratio are
the consequences of absorption, scattering and marine-snow dominating the
properties of water. In order to inspect underwater infrastructure like dam
walls or offshore wind farms image enhancement or image restoration is crucial. In this technical report a model for underwater light propagation is derived. The presented model has the ability to describe many effects on image
degradation in underwater imaging, e.g. low contrast, brightening, decrease
of signal-to-noise-ratio and color-shift.

1 Introduction

Offshore wind farms, dam walls and other infrastructure facilities underwater are
usually inspected manually by human divers. The disadvantages of this approach
are well known: It is dangerous, expensive, time consuming and does not even allow complete assessments. Consequently it is necessary to automate the inspection
under water. This requires imaging sensors that are able to detect the infrastructure and their inherent defects. Optical imaging sensors benefit other sensors in
one crucial point: The resulting images are intuitive evaluable by the human observer. However, these sensors provide hardly usable results under water. The
high wavelength-dependent light absorption and scattering as well as disturbing
suspended particles produce a decrease in contrast, blurred and noisy images.

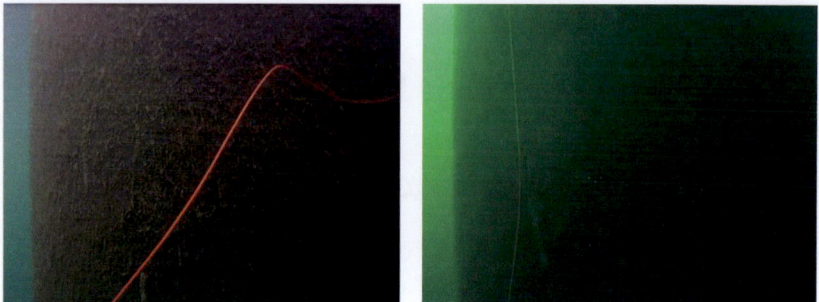

Figure 1.1: These images were captured in a catchment lake. Image quality degrades with the distance to the object. Only few meters unter water surface, details of underwater buildings can be inspected hardly (right image).

1.1 Problems of underwater imaging

The poor visibility under water is mainly caused by absorption, scattering and particles. Each cause produces specific image degradations.

Absorption The energy of the light field reduces gradually by the water and its inherent particles. A light beam that is emitted into water decreases continuously. This results in low image intensities, high exposure times and in the need of intense illumination.

Scattering Light rays are scattered by water and its inherited particles, i.e. they change their direction stochastically. Two different imaging effects were caused by scattering. At the one hand light rays were fanned, which results as blurred images. At the other hand ambient light is scattered into the direction of the camera. Thus, the contrast decreases with the distance to the object.

Particles Particles under water are often denoted as marine snow. Parts of scene objects are covered by such particles. Particles within water diminish the signal-to-noise-ratio (SNR). For all image restoration tasks the SNR limits the possible quality of restored images. As a last consequence the density of particles in water determines the capabilities of optical underwater imaging systems.

1.2   Contribution

This technical report presents a derivation of a model for the underwater imaging process. The derived model is able to describe many image degradation effects caused by wavelength dependent absorption and scattering. Section 2 gives a short insight into radiance quantities and mechanisms of light transportation. In section 3 the model is deduced and compared with another model of image processing.

2   Elements of Radiative Transfer

For understanding the derived Model of light transfer and imaging process, some physical quantities and light interaction mechanisms have to be explained first. The quantities described here, are in detail the radiant flux, the irradiance, the radiant intensity and the radiance. Relevant mechanisms of light interaction under water are absorption, scattering and reflection [Mob94, Ish78, Cha60].

2.1   Radiometry – Quantities

Radiant Flux: The radiant flux Φ is the measure of radiation power passing a surface. Its unit is Watt $[W]$. If the surface equals to a sphere around a light source, the corresponding radiant flux gives the emitted power of the light source.

Irradiance: The quantity of irradiance E describes the density of radiant flux Φ per area element $\mathrm{d}A$. Thus, irradiance can be written as

$$E = \frac{\mathrm{d}\Phi}{\mathrm{d}A},$$

with its unit $\left[\frac{W}{m^2}\right]$.

Radiant Intensity: Whereas irradiance is the density of radiated power related to an area element $\mathrm{d}A$, radiant intensity I is the density of radiated power related to a solid angle element $\mathrm{d}\omega$. Therefore, radiant intensity can be defined as

$$I = \frac{\mathrm{d}\Phi}{\mathrm{d}\omega}$$

with its unit $\left[\frac{W}{sr}\right]$, where sr denotes the unit of a solid angle.

Radiance: Another quantity of radiometry is the radiance. It gives the best association to a single light ray at a certain position in a certain direction. The radiance L is the area-projection of the density of power coming from an area element $\mathrm{d}A$ radiated into a solid angle element $\mathrm{d}\omega$.

$$L = \frac{\mathrm{d}^2\Phi}{\mathrm{d}A\,\mathrm{d}\omega\,\cos(\theta)},$$

where θ denotes the angle of the direction of the light ray referring to the area element $\mathrm{d}A$. The relation between radiance, irradiance and radiant intensity can be described by

$$L = \frac{\mathrm{d}I}{\mathrm{d}A\,\cos(\theta)} \qquad L = \frac{\mathrm{d}E}{\mathrm{d}\omega\,\cos(\theta)} \tag{2.1}$$

2.2 Radiometry – Light Interaction Mechanisms

Absorption: Absorption is caused by annihilation of photons of the radiance beam and conversion of radiant energy to non-radiant energy. The change in radiance while crossing a volume element due to absorption is proportional to the incident radiance.

$$\mathrm{d}L = -aL$$

The proportionality factor a is called absorption coefficient.

Scattering: A photon can be deflected by a particle into directions diverging from origin direction. This process is called scattering. Scattering of a light ray with direction $\boldsymbol{r}'$ into direction $\boldsymbol{r}$ can be defined as

$$\beta\left(\boldsymbol{r}' \to \boldsymbol{r}\right) = \frac{\mathrm{d}I(\boldsymbol{r})}{E\left(\boldsymbol{r}'\right)\mathrm{d}V},$$

where $\mathrm{d}V$ denotes a volume element of scattering medium. The quantity

$$b = \int_{\Omega} \beta(\boldsymbol{r}(\omega))\,\mathrm{d}\omega \tag{2.2}$$

is called scattering coefficient. Here $\boldsymbol{r}(\omega)$ denotes the direction of light ray corresponding to the solid angle $\omega \in \Omega$. The relation between radiance and scattering can be described by

$$\mathrm{d}I(\boldsymbol{r}) = \mathrm{d}V \int_{\Omega} L(\boldsymbol{r}')\beta(\boldsymbol{r}' \to \boldsymbol{r}(\omega))\,\mathrm{d}\omega \tag{2.3}$$

Reflection: Reflection is the change of direction of a radiant beam on a surface. The bidirectional reflactance distribution function (BRDF) describes the outgoing radiance $L(r)$ with respect to the ingoing irradiance $E(r')$. If the surface is lambertian the BRDF is constant with respect to the directions of the radiant beam, the BRDF is then called reflectance coefficient ρ.

3 Concept

In this section the model of imaging under water will be explained. First of all the scene and its setup will be described, then the model will be derived.

3.1 Geometric Scene

In the derived Model of underwater imaging the scene consists of two different coordinate systems. The world coordinate system lies in the three dimensional space $\mathbb{R}^3$ an contains scene objects as well as the model of the camera. The image plane, subset of $\mathbb{R}^2$, contains its own coordinate system. The camera is modeled as pinhole camera, with the projection center o. Therefore, the imaging process is a case of projective transformation.

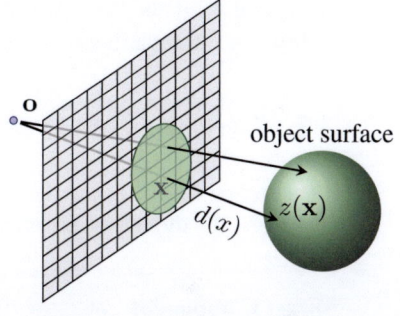

Figure 3.1: Illustration of the geometric scene

The coordinate, henceforth referred to as $x \in \mathbb{R}^2$, lies in the image plane and denotes the position of the pixel of camera sensor. $x_w \in \mathbb{R}^3$ denotes the coordinates of the point x in world coordinates. The sight line corresponding to x is the line in $\mathbb{R}^3$ containing the projection center o and the point x_w. If this line intersects object surfaces the intersection point with the least distance to the camera is denoted as $z(x)$. This point is unambiguous. The set of points $z(x)$ represents a two dimensional manifold embedded in the three dimensional space $\mathbb{R}^3$. The distance from the projection center to the imaged object surface is denoted as $d(x) = \|o - z(x)\|$.

3.2 Radiometric Scene

The irradiation on the surface $z(x)$ is denoted by $E^{(\lambda)}(x)$, where λ is the wavelength of the irradiance. The surface is assumed to be lambertian, thus, the reflectance properties of the surface can be described by the reflactance coefficient $\rho^{(\lambda)}$.

The spectral surface radiation $L_z^{(\lambda)}(x)$ denotes the radiation referring to the wavelength λ at point $z(x)$ with the direction $\frac{o-z(x)}{\|o-z(x)\|}$. The line composed of the surface point $z(x)$ and the direction $\frac{o-z(x)}{\|o-z(x)\|}$ is equal to the sight line through x_w.

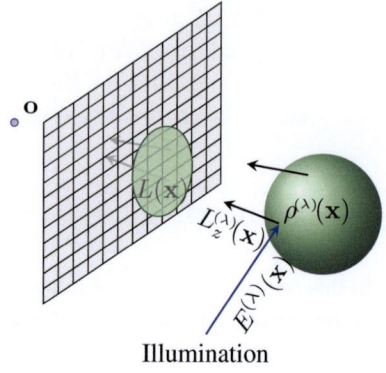

Figure 3.2: Illustration of the radiometric scene

3.3 Derivation of the model

This section describes the derivation of the presented model. It is partitioned into two parts, the direct component and the indirect component

Direct Component

First of all the direct component of underwater imaging process is described. The direct component denominates the light ray which came from the surface point $z(x)$ and reach the image plane at the corresponding image point x without beeing scattered. The direct component consists of radiance on a surface point $z(x)$ passing the medium water. During the transition through the column of water it will be attenuated by absorption and scattered into another direction. This attenuation can be described by the Beer-Lambert law

$$L^{(\lambda)}(x) = L_z^{(\lambda)}(x)\, e^{-c^{(\lambda)}d(x)},$$

where $c^{(\lambda)} = a^{(\lambda)} + b^{(\lambda)}$ is the sum of the absorption coefficient and the scattering coefficient and is assumed to be constant over the field of view. The radiance $L_z^{(\lambda)}(x)$ on the surface point x is caused by the ambiance light near the surface and the surface inherent reflection coefficient $\rho^{(\lambda)}x$.

$$L_z^{(\lambda)}(x) = \rho^{(\lambda)}(x)E^{(\lambda)}(x)$$

Thus, the radiance $L^{(\lambda)}(\boldsymbol{x})$ on the image plane caused by the direct component can be calculated by

$$L^{(\lambda)}(\boldsymbol{x}) = \rho^{(\lambda)}(\boldsymbol{x}) E^{(\lambda)}(\boldsymbol{x}) \, e^{-c^{(\lambda)} d(\boldsymbol{x})}. \tag{3.1}$$

Indirect Component – Backscattering

The indirect component or backscatter component of underwater imaging is the part of light, which is scattered by the medium water at a scene point in the field of view into the direction of projection center $\boldsymbol{o}$.

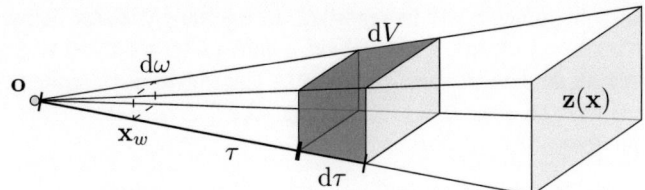

Figure 3.3: Backscattering of a volume element on sight line

In the following the radiance reaching the image point $\boldsymbol{x}_w$ coming from volume element dV (see figure 3.3) will be discussed. Applying the Beer-Lambert law leads to

$$dL^{(\lambda)}(\boldsymbol{x}) = L^{(\lambda)}(\tau) e^{-c^{(\lambda)}\tau}.$$

From (2.1) and (2.3) it follows that

$$\begin{aligned}
dL^{(\lambda)}(\boldsymbol{x}) &= L^{(\lambda)}(\tau) e^{-c^{(\lambda)}\tau} \\
&= \frac{dI^{(\lambda)}(\tau, \boldsymbol{r}) e^{-c^{(\lambda)}\tau}}{dA} \\
&= \frac{dV \int_\Omega L^{(\lambda)}(\boldsymbol{r}') \beta^{(\lambda)}(\boldsymbol{r}' \to \boldsymbol{r}(\omega)) \, d\omega \, e^{-c^{(\lambda)}\tau}}{dA} \\
&= d\tau \int_\Omega L^{(\lambda)}(\boldsymbol{r}') \beta^{(\lambda)}(\boldsymbol{r}' \to \boldsymbol{r}(\omega)) \, d\omega \, e^{-c^{(\lambda)}\tau}
\end{aligned}$$

Assuming a spatial constant ambient illumination, this leads with (2.2) to

$$dL^{(\lambda)}(\boldsymbol{x}) = b^{(\lambda)} k^{(\lambda)} e^{-c^{(\lambda)}\tau} \, d\tau.$$

Hence, integrating over τ gives the backscattering component

$$L^{(\lambda)}(\boldsymbol{x}) = \int_0^{d(\boldsymbol{x})} b^{(\lambda)} k^{(\lambda)} e^{-c^{(\lambda)}\tau} \, d\tau = \frac{b^{(\lambda)}}{c^{(\lambda)}} k^{(\lambda)} \left(1 - e^{-c^{(\lambda)} d(\boldsymbol{x})}\right). \tag{3.2}$$

Radiance Model

Because of linearity of light transportation all light components can be added to the total radiance on the image plane. Summation of equation (3.1) and (3.2) leads to the overall radiance Model

$$L^{(\lambda)}(\boldsymbol{x}) = \rho^{(\lambda)}(\boldsymbol{x})E^{(\lambda)}(\boldsymbol{x})\,\mathrm{e}^{-c^{(\lambda)}d(\boldsymbol{x})} + \frac{b^{(\lambda)}}{c^{(\lambda)}}k^{(\lambda)}\left(1 - \mathrm{e}^{-c^{(\lambda)}d(\boldsymbol{x})}\right). \qquad (3.3)$$

Imaging Process

Now the imaging process will be regarded. Irradiation incide the camera on sensor chip at $\boldsymbol{x}$ cause an electric potential on a camera sensor pixel $\boldsymbol{u}$ depending on the wavelength dependent sensitivity $\Lambda^{(\lambda)}$. The potential generated by radiation is collected over an area $A(\boldsymbol{u})$ and a time slice $[t_0, t_0 + \Delta t]$. This leads to the imaging process

$$g^{(\lambda)}(\boldsymbol{u}) = \int_{t_0}^{t_0+\Delta t} \int_{A(\boldsymbol{u})} \int_{\Omega(\boldsymbol{u})} \Lambda^{(\lambda)}L^{(\lambda)}(\boldsymbol{x}_w, \boldsymbol{r}(\omega))cos(\theta(\boldsymbol{x},\omega))\,\mathrm{d}\omega\,\mathrm{d}\boldsymbol{x}\,\mathrm{d}t,$$
$$(3.4)$$

where $\theta(\boldsymbol{x},\omega)$ is the angle of incident light beam on the sensor chip surface. Assuming a pinhole camera model, constant incident radiation on a pixel $\boldsymbol{u}$ and a static scene over the time interval $[t_0, t_0 + \Delta t]$ the equation in (3.4) reduces to

$$g^{(\lambda)}(\boldsymbol{u}) \propto L^{(\lambda)}(\boldsymbol{x})cos(\theta(\boldsymbol{x})). \qquad (3.5)$$

Thus, equation (3.3) and (3.5) leads to

$$\frac{g^{(\lambda)}(\boldsymbol{u})}{\cos(\theta(\boldsymbol{x}))} \propto \rho^{(\lambda)}(\boldsymbol{x})E^{(\lambda)}(\boldsymbol{x})\,\mathrm{e}^{-c^{(\lambda)}d(\boldsymbol{x})} + \frac{b^{(\lambda)}}{c^{(\lambda)}}k^{(\lambda)}\left(1 - \mathrm{e}^{-c^{(\lambda)}d(\boldsymbol{x})}\right). \qquad (3.6)$$

3.4   Discussion of the Model

In many image processing tasks [HST10, LLW08] the process of imaging is described with a simple signal model

$$g(\boldsymbol{x}) = s(\boldsymbol{x})t(\boldsymbol{x}) + \alpha \cdot (1 - t(\boldsymbol{x})), \qquad (3.7)$$

where $s(\boldsymbol{x})$ is the signal, $t(\boldsymbol{x})$ is a function depending on $\boldsymbol{x}$ with $t(\boldsymbol{x}) \in [0,1]$ and a constant α. Associating the image $g(\boldsymbol{x})$ from (3.7) with the cosine calibrated image $\frac{g^{(\lambda)}(\boldsymbol{u})}{\cos(\theta(\boldsymbol{x}))}$ from (3.6) both signal models are equal. Hereby, the signal can be described as $s(\boldsymbol{x}) = \rho^{(\lambda)}(\boldsymbol{x})E^{(\lambda)}(\boldsymbol{x})$, $t(\boldsymbol{x}) = \mathrm{e}^{-c^{(\lambda)}d(\boldsymbol{x})}$ and $\alpha = \frac{b^{(\lambda)}}{c^{(\lambda)}}k^{(\lambda)}$. Thus, many mechanisms of image processing, laplacian soft matting for example [LLW08], can be taken into account for underwater image processing.

Range dependent loss of contrast

The intensity of the signal $s(\boldsymbol{x})$ decrease exponentially with the distance to the imaging projection center. Where the backscatter component increase up to a constant value dependent on the properties of water

$$\lim_{d(\boldsymbol{x})\to\infty} \rho^{(\lambda)}(\boldsymbol{x})E^{(\lambda)}(\boldsymbol{x})\,\mathrm{e}^{-c^{(\lambda)}d(\boldsymbol{x})} = 0$$

$$\lim_{d(\boldsymbol{x})\to\infty} \frac{b^{(\lambda)}}{c^{(\lambda)}}k^{(\lambda)}\left(1 - \mathrm{e}^{-c^{(\lambda)}d(\boldsymbol{x})}\right) = \frac{b^{(\lambda)}}{c^{(\lambda)}}k^{(\lambda)}.$$

This causes a loss of contrast, related to the distance of imaged object surface. As a consequence signal-to-noise-ratio decrease with the distance to the imaged object.

At the other hand the decrease of signal intensity and the increase of imaged backscatter component can be used to estimate the distance to the object surface. On positions $\boldsymbol{x}$, where the signal is close to zero, only the backscatter component is imaged. With the knowledge of the water properties, the distance to the object can be calculated very easily.

3.5   Color-Shift

Another effect on underwater image degradation is the occurring color-shift. In most underwater images the results are very bluish or greenish. This is caused by the wavelength dependent absorption $a^{(\lambda)}$ and scattering coefficient $b^{(\lambda)}$ of water. The absorption coefficient of red components of light spectra are quiet higher, than the absorption coefficients of blue or green components, thus the imaged results are bluish. In turbid water the absorption of blue components of light are decreased by algal or mineral particles, and therefore the images are greenish. The deeper the object, the fewer the red amount of natural light reaches the object surface. As a consequence of these, artificial lighting will be indispensable at greater depths.

4   Conclusion

In this technical report an imaging model for optical underwater systems was derived. The model bases on physical laws and is able to describe many of the phenomena of image degradation of underwater imaging, e.g. color-shift, loss of contrast, brightening and increasing signal-to-noise-ratio. It is shown, that the model equals to the model of soft matting and other image models, thus, methods like laplacian soft matting can be adapted to underwater imaging.

Otherwise, the model can be used for different tasks in image processing, e.g. image restoration, depth estimation and estimation of water inherent properties.

Bibliography

[Cha60]   S. Chandrasekhar. *Radiative transfer*. Dover, New York, 1960.

[HST10]   Kaiming He, Jian Sun, and Xiaoou Tang. Single Image Haze Removal Using Dark Channel Prior. *IEEE Transactions on Pattern Analysis and Machine Intelligence*, 2010.

[Ish78]   Akira Ishimaru. *Wave propagation and scattering in random media*. Academic Pr., New York, 1978.

[LLW08]   Anat Levin, Dani Lischinski, and Yair Weiss. A Closed-Form Solution to Natural Image Matting. *Pattern Analysis and Machine Intelligence, IEEE Transactions on*, 2008, 2008.

[Mob94]   Curtis D. Mobley. *Light and water: Radiative transfer in natural waters*. Academic Press, San Diego, 1994.

Extending Object-Oriented World Modeling for Adaptive Open-World Modeling

Achim Kuwertz

Vision and Fusion Laboratory
Institute for Anthropomatics
Karlsruhe Institute of Technology (KIT), Germany
achim.kuwertz@kit.edu

Technical Report IES-2012-06

Abstract:

In this technical report, details for extending the Object-Oriented World Model (OOWM) to an open-world modeling approach by adaptive management of its background knowledge are proposed. In general, a world model can serve as a central component in autonomous and cognitive systems for integrating, storing and disseminating information about an observed environment. Thus, a world model creates an abstract, simplified representation of an observed real-world domain. For allowing high-level information processing on a semantic layer, representations of real-world entities can be semantically enriched by domain models. In general, a domain model contains only a fixed number of a priori defined concepts from a closed world. However, in many real-life applications, the considered environment is not closed. For coping with changing environments, a cognitive system must be equipped with an adaptive world model able to adjust to an observed open environment. This technical report proposes details on how the OOWM can be extended for adaptive world modeling by continuously evaluating the quality of its domain model in comparison to observed information.

1 Introduction

A world model provides a structured way to organize information that is available about an environment of interest. Such information often is a prerequisite for those systems and humans that, in some way, have to interact with or operate in that environment. A world model can support tasks like the generation of operational pictures or the assessment of situations, thus allowing humans to make well-informed decisions or enable autonomous system like service robots to fulfill their jobs. To

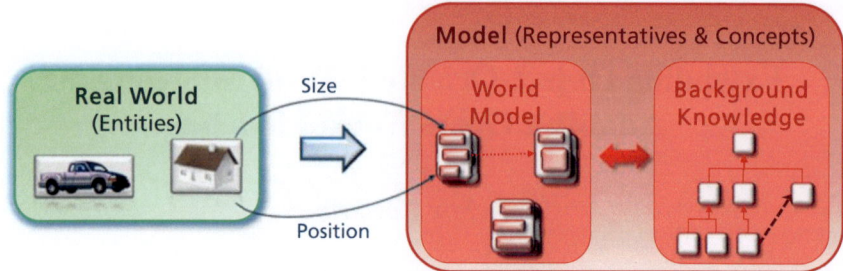

Figure 1.1: Object-Oriented World Modeling. Real-world entities are observed by sensors and the acquired observation information gets stored in the World Model as information objects called representatives. In Background Knowledge, a priori modeled concept classes for these objects are defined as well as static properties.

support such tasks, a world model has to handle different kinds of information, like a priori knowledge about static properties of an environment of interest as well as current data on dynamic properties acquired by sensor observations. All this information has to be represented in a consistent manner, allowing to update and fuse established information with new data. A proven solution to this tasks of managing environmental information is given by the Object-Oriented World Model (OOWM) [GHB08b], which has been successfully applied in domains like autonomous systems [BKFB12b] or situation assessment [FB10b].

1.1   Object-Oriented World Modeling

The OOWM is a world model which represents environment information on real-world entities in an object-oriented way. It constitutes a probabilistic data and information fusion framework which is able to integrate observation information from heterogeneous sensing systems with a priori information on a given application domain. Designed as an information hub, the OOWM can provide higher level processing modules, like situation assessment or action planing modules, with consistently integrated information representing the current state of an observed environment. For handling the different kinds of stored information, the OOWM consists of the two components depicted in Figure 1.1. The dynamic modeling part, called the World Model, stores acquired observation information on the attributes of real-world entities, like their position and size. Observed entities are represented as sets of observed attributes $\mathcal{A}_R := \{A_1, A_2, \ldots, A_n\}, n \in \mathbb{N}$ called representatives. Each attribute observation $A_i \in \mathcal{A}_R$ is represented by a probability distribution $p_{A_i}(a)$ describing the degree of belief (*DoB*) in the observed value. For representing discrete attributes, i.e., nominally, ordinally or absolutely scaled attributes, discrete probability distributions $p_A^d : \mathcal{S}_A \mapsto [0, 1]$ with $|\mathcal{S}_A| \leq \infty$, $\sum_{a \in \mathcal{S}_A} p_A^d(a) = 1$, are employed. Continuous attributes, i.e., interval scaled or ratio scaled attributes, are represented by continuous distributions $p_A^c : \mathcal{D}_A \subseteq \mathbb{R} \mapsto [0, \infty)$ with $\int_{\mathcal{D}_A} p_A^c(a)\, \mathrm{d}a = 1$, in most cases, Gaussian mixture distributions. A priori knowledge about the application environment is modeled in the second OOWM component, the Background Knowledge. This Background Knowledge results from a manual conceptualization process, in which each relevant environment entity is modeled as an object-oriented concept class C characterized by its set of concept attributes $\mathcal{A}_C := \{A_1, A_2, \ldots, A_m\}$. These attributes are again represented by probability distributions $p_{A_c}(a)$. The concept classes in Background Knowledge are organized in hierarchies $\mathcal{H}$ of concept classes capturing the subclass relations of the modeled real-world entities.

1.2   Adaptive World Modeling

The Background Knowledge enables the OOWM to classify observed real-world entities based on their attribute values, and, if needed, derive additional, yet unobserved information. For this classification to work, representatives have to be linked to concept classes, which in case of the OOWM is achieved by a probabilistic classification mechanism associating representatives R to concepts C by a conditional probability distribution $p(C|R)$. The concepts in Background Knowledge are modeled a priori and manually, and thus, only a limited and closed part of the application environment can be considered. Yet, during OOWM operation, it is possible to encounter unmodeled real-world entities, which in consequence, cannot be classified according to the predefined concept classes. In order to cope with such circumstances and allow for an open world modeling, an adaptive approach for managing the information represented in the OOWM Background Knowledge is necessary. The conception of such an adaptive approach to open world modeling will be presented in this report. For adaptive modeling, methods for evaluating the quality of Background Knowledge with respect to the representatives in the World Model are needed. Besides judging the ability of Background Knowledge to explain the observed entities, procedures for adjusting Background Knowledge to the observed world are necessary. In Section 2, an overview of concept learning and approaches for the automatic generation of concept hierarichies is given and presented within in common notation formalism. Section 3 extends this formalism the model evaluation of Background Knowledge and presents an approach to adaptive open-world modeling for the OOWM as information management problem.

2   Concept Learning and Taxonomy

In this section, an overview of existing approaches to concept learning and taxonomy generation is given. The presented approaches will be compared within a common formalization. For this purpose, suppose that a number of entities $\mathcal{E} = \{E_1, E_2, \ldots, E_k\}$ is given, each of which is characterized by observed features represented as a subset of attributes from $\mathcal{A} = \{A_1, A_2, \ldots, A_m\}$. One goal of the presented approaches is to group the entities in $\mathcal{E}$ into classes $C_i \in \mathcal{C}$ with $C_i \subset \mathcal{E}$. Another goal is to find a conceptual description for each created class C_i.

2.1   Learning from Examples and Concept Learning

The task of learning from examples, in contrast to learning from observations, can in general be described by being given a set of training data $\{(\bar{A}_1, C_1'), (\bar{A}_2, C_2'), \ldots, (\bar{A}_n, C_n')\}$, where the $\bar{A}_i = [A_{i_1}, A_{i_2}, \ldots, A_{i_l}]^T$ with $A_{i_j} \in \mathcal{A}$ represent the observable part of the data (here denoted as vector of attributes in the common formalism) and the C_i' represent a valuation of this data. If a functional relationship between the $\bar{A}_i$- and C_i'-values is to be discovered, this task is either called regression (in the statistics domain) or supervised learning (in the machine learning domain) [Grü07]. The more special case where the C'-values are restricted to some finite set $\mathcal{C}$ is called classification, or, in computational learning theory, concept learning.

The classical approach to concept learning [Mit97] is concerned with learning concept descriptions for predefined classes C_i of entities from $\mathcal{E}$. A concept is regarded as a function mapping attribute values $\bar{A}_i$ of discrete attributes to a boolean value indicating concept membership. In this case, the set of entities $\mathcal{E}$ is defined by the outer product over the range of the considered attributes in $\mathcal{A}$. Concepts are described as hypotheses, i.e., the conjunction of restrictions on allowed attribute values like allowing just one specific, a set of or any value for an attribute.

The task of classical concept learning consists of finding a hypothesis for each class C_i that matches the training data. This task can be performed as a directed search in hypotheses space by exploiting a preexisting ordering relation, the so-called general-to-specific ordering of hypotheses. A hypothesis thereby is more general than another if its set of allowed instances is a superset to the set of instances belonging to the other hypothesis. Based on this ordering, several concept learning algorithms have been developed, including the well-known version space algorithm [Mit79].

2.2 Numerical Taxonomy

The area of numerical taxonomy [Sok66] is a subfield to the research in taxonomy, the science concerning classification in general. It has been successfully employed in biological taxonomy for extracting and defining groups and hierarchical relationships of biological organisms based on characteristic features [MS57]. It was developed as an approach to generating non-subjective classification schemes, which are based on well-described procedures, for tasks involving large numbers of features intractable for manual handling.

The basic problem to be solved is the following: given a number of objects, which are described by discrete characteristic features, a natural grouping of the objects and a hierarchy of these groups is search for [Sok66]. Natural thereby means that objects within the same group should be more similar to each other than objects sorted into different groups - an objective shared with methods for cluster analysis. Formulated within the common description formalism introduced above, the basic problem of numerical taxonomy can be stated as follows: given a set of observed entities $\mathcal{E}$ described by discrete attributes $A_i \in \mathcal{A}$, a structure $\mathcal{H}$ for hierarchically ordering these observations into groups (or classes) $C_i \subset \mathcal{E}$ is searched for.

The approach taken by numerical taxonomy for solving this problem is presented next. In a first step, pairwise similarity scores are computed for all entities to be classified, based on discrete attribute values which represent their respective features. For computing the similarity score, several correlation or distance measures can be employed, which will be examined in detail below. As a result, a similarity matrix can be plotted. A reordering of the objects at the matrix axes according to their levels of similarity allows to create a first classification into 'groups'. A more accurate classification, represented as a dendogram, can be reached by employing hierarchical clustering algorithms. Several approaches to hierarchical clustering exist, differing e.g. in design choices like

- how many entities can be contained in a cluster (pairwise vs. variable grouping [SM58]),

- how the similarity of clusters is calculated based on their contained entities (single-linkage (minimum distance) vs. average vs. overall linkage (maximum distance) [Sok66], or

- how the entities contained in a cluster are weighted in similarity calculation (weighted vs. unweighted calculation) [SM58].

The general approach to creating a taxonomy of groups $\mathcal{H} := (C_1^H, C_2^H, \cdots, C_h^H)$ with either $C_i^H \supset C_j^H$ or $C_i^H \cap C_j^H = \emptyset$ for $i < j$, as described in [SM58], constitutes an iterative method which in each iteration creates a new hierarchy level. Each iteration begins by sorting the pairwise similarities $d(E_i, E_j)$ for all considered entities in descending order. Then, a cluster is created by joining the two most similar entities into a group C^H and continuously adding to this group those entities being most similar (in average) to the entities contained in the group. This goes on as long as adding an entity to the group does not significantly decrease the average similarity of the group $\bar{d}(C^H) := \sum_{E_i \neq E_j \in C^H} d(E_i, E_j)$. If a significant decrease occurs, no more entities are added to the current group and a new cluster is created with the two entities being pairwise next most similar, according to the initial sorting, and filled as just described. An iteration ends when no more new clusters can be created - this occurs when at least one of the entities of a new cluster is already contained in another cluster created during this iteration. Which decrease in overall similarity is considered significant depends on the application domain and has to be determined empirically.

In the next iteration, each cluster C_i^H is represented by a proxy entity subsuming all its contained entities and a new similarity score is calculated for this representative and all the remaining entities C_j^H according to

$$d(C_i^H, C_j^H) = \frac{\sum_{E_i \in C_i^H} \sum_{E_j \in C_j^H} d(E_i, E_j)}{\sqrt{|C_i^H| + 2 \cdot \bar{d}(C_i^H)} + \sqrt{|C_j^H| + 2 \cdot \bar{d}(C_j^H)}} \ .$$

In the special case where C_j^H is not a group but a single entity, the summand $\sqrt{|C_j^H| + 2 \cdot \bar{d}(C_j^H)}$ is set to 0. Then the iteration proceeds as described above. Using a iteration-based grouping method allows for creating clusters that contain more than two entities (called variable grouping). It furthermore allows to define a clear notion of level for the resulting hierarchy in contrast to what results from a pair grouping approach. A well-known special case for pair-based clustering is the so-called Unweighted Pair Grouping Method with Arithmetic Averages (UPGMA) [PAM01] method, a kind of agglomerative hierarchical clustering [HTF09].

Besides creating a taxonomy, the main aspect of numerical taxonomy concerns determining the similarity of entities. Over time, a lot of different similarity scores for comparing entities based on their attributes have been developed. These measures can be distinguished by either being pure association measures, which rate similarity only based on which attributes are defined for entities (ignoring attribute values), or by being correlation or distance measures rating similarity as the degree of correlation between attribute values or as a distance between the values. In addition, combined measures exist. Given the sets of attribute values

$\mathcal{A}_j = \{A_{j_1}, A_{j_2}, \ldots, A_{j_{n_j}}\} \subseteq \mathcal{A}$ and $\mathcal{A}_k$ for the entities E_j and E_k, the similarity $d(E_j, E_k)$ can be for example determined by using one of the following similarity scores. [Cha07] analyzes these measures for use with probability density functions.

1. Association measures:

   - Matching Coefficient [SM58]

   $$d(E_j, E_k) = \frac{1}{m} \cdot \left(|\mathcal{A}_j \cap \mathcal{A}_k| + |\mathcal{A} \setminus (\mathcal{A}_j \cup \mathcal{A}_k)| \right)$$

   - Sørenson-Dice (e.g. [Maq03])

   $$d(E_j, E_k) = \frac{2 \cdot |\mathcal{A}_j \cap \mathcal{A}_k|}{|\mathcal{A}_j| + |\mathcal{A}_k|}$$

   - Tanimoto (e.g. [Maq03])

   $$d(E_j, E_k) = \frac{|\mathcal{A}_j \cap \mathcal{A}_k| + |\mathcal{A} \setminus (\mathcal{A}_j \cup \mathcal{A}_k)|}{m + |(\mathcal{A}_j \cup \mathcal{A}_j) \setminus (\mathcal{A}_j \cap \mathcal{A}_m)|}$$

2. Correlation measures:

   - Product-moment correlation (used in [SM58])

   $$d(E_j, E_k) = \frac{m \cdot \sum a_{i_j} a_{i_k} - \sum a_{i_j} \sum a_{i_k}}{\sqrt{m \cdot \sum a_{i_j}^2 - (\sum a_{i_j})^2} \sqrt{m \cdot \sum a_{i_k}^2 - (\sum a_{i_k})^2}}$$

3. Distance measures:

   - Normalized Euclidean Distance (used in [RS65])

   $$d(E_j, E_k) = \frac{1}{\sqrt{m}} \cdot \sqrt{\sum_{i=1,\ldots,m} (a_{i_j} - a_{i_k})^2}$$

   - Canberra Distance (e.g. [Maq03]):

   $$d(E_j, E_k) = \sum_{i=1,\ldots,m} \frac{|a_{i_j} - a_{i_k}|}{|a_{i_j}| + |a_{i_k}|}$$

4. Combined Measures:

   - General Similarity Coefficient (Gower, cited in [PAM01])

   $$d(E_j, E_k) = \frac{1}{\sum_{i=1,\ldots,m} \delta_{i_j i_k}} \cdot \sum_{i=1,\ldots,m} \delta_{i_j i_k} \cdot \left(1 - \frac{|a_{i_j} - a_{i_k}|}{|S_{A_i}|} \right)$$

3   Concept Learning as Information Management

After reviewing methods and approaches from literature and related work for rating the similarity of attributes and entities as well as creating hierarchies in Section 2, this section now is concerned with how to put such methods to use adaptive world modeling. The approach presented below considers extending the OOWM Background Knowledge by learning new concept definitions as an information management problem. Within this approach to adaptive management of model knowledge, several subtasks have to be addressed. One important subtask is the evaluation of the quality of the knowledge model, reflecting how well OOWM Background Knowledge is able to represent the entities so far observed in the real world. If model quality is insufficient, Background Knowledge has to be adjusted and extended as necessary. Model adjustment and extension are the two other important subtasks of adaptive world modeling. These subtasks include the creation of new concept classes as well as adjusting the attributes and attribute values of existing concepts and their hierarchical organization.

In this report, the main focus for adaptive world modeling will be set on the model evaluation task dealing with the problem of how to evaluate the quality of OOWM Background knowledge with respect to the real-world information observed to this point of time. Since the primary purpose of OOWM Background Knowledge is to allow a classification of observed entities, i.e., a mapping of representatives to concept classes, the correspondence of a priori modeled knowledge to representatives is a main factor for rating OOWM knowledge quality. In addition to this classification related correspondence, the complexity of Background Knowledge, reflecting how specific or general the represented knowledge is, constitutes a second influencing for model evaluation. Thus, the parameters determining the quality of Background Knowledge in this approach are the set of representatives $\mathcal{R}$, including all observed attributes $\mathcal{A}_R$, as well as the set of concept classes $\mathcal{C}$ in Background Knowledge and the probabilistic association $p(C|R)$ of each representative $R \in \mathcal{R}$ to a concept $C \in \mathcal{C}$. For a measure $Q(\cdot)$ rating the overall quality of OOWM knowledge, all these parameters have to be taken into account.

3.1   Criteria for Model Evaluation and Adaption

When rating the quality of a model for explaining given data, different criteria or principles can be employed for selecting one model over another, for example the Bayesian Information Criterion [Sch78]. For implementing a measure of model quality in adaptive world modeling, an approach based on the principle of Minimum Description Length (*MDL*, e.g. [Grü07]) was chosen. MDL aims at selecting models which allow to represent observed data with a description of minimal encoding length by extracting regularities from the data. These regularities, when formalized into models, can then be used to represent the data in a compressed way by only describing the deviations of observed data from the model and, additionally, the model itself. A simple approach to this principle is crude MDL as presented by [Grü07]. Here, a two-part term $L = L(D|M) + L(M)$ determines the description length L of a model M for given data D. The first term $L(D|M)$ in crude MDL specifies the description length needed to represent the data D based on the model M, and the second term $L(M)$ specifies the description length of the model. Following this general idea of crude MDL, a measure for rating the model quality of OOWM Background Knowledge can be designed according to $Q(\mathcal{R}, \mathcal{C}) = L(\mathcal{R}|\mathcal{C}) + L(\mathcal{C})$, where the concepts $\mathcal{C}$ in Background Knowledge constitute the model and the representatives $\mathcal{R}$ in the World Model depict the so far observed real-world data. In this measure, the term $L(\mathcal{C})$ rates the complexity of OOWM Background Knowledge, and the term $L(\mathcal{R}|\mathcal{C})$ specifies the correspondence of observed representative information to modeled concepts. Including model complexity in this measure implements a constraint used in many kinds of classification tasks for preventing the model from overfitting to observed information data during model adaptation. This allows to maintain the ability of Background Knowledge for generalizing from observed information.

3.2   A Measure of Model Complexity

As one part of model quality, the complexity of Background Knowledge has to be measured. The overall complexity of OOWM Background Knowledge $L(\mathcal{C})$ depends on the complexity of the set of modeled concepts: $L(\mathcal{C}) := \sum_{C \in \mathcal{C}} L(C)$. Modeled concepts are rated to be more complex the more specific they are, which depends on their attributes $A_c \in \mathcal{A}_C : L(C) = \sum_{A_c \in \mathcal{A}_C} L(A_c)$. A concept is thus rated more specific the more attributes it is described with and the more specific the description of each attribute is. As cumulative measure for rating OOWM Background Knowledge complexity based on the DoB distributions of attributes

$$L(\mathcal{C}) := \sum_{C \in \mathcal{C}} \sum_{A_c \in \mathcal{A}_C} L\left(p_{A_c}(a)\right)$$

results. The specificity of DoB distributions $L\left(p_{A_c}(a)\right)$ rates the concentration of features to only certain values of the distribution support. As a specific measure, Shannon entropy $H(\cdot)$ can be employed for this purpose. For discrete attributes A^d, the Shannon entropy of the distribution $p_A^d(a)$ is given by

$$H(A^d) = - \sum_{a \in S_A} p_A^d \cdot \log(p_A^d(a)) \ .$$

As an information-theoretic measure, Shannon entropy is greater the less concentrated a distribution is. Assuming a limited support for the DoB distribution, given by the set $\mathcal{S}_A$ of attribute values, Shannon entropy $H(A^d)$ can be employed to rate attribute specificity according to $L(A^d) = \log(|\mathcal{S}_A|) - H(A^d)$. This measure explicitly accounts for the support of an attribute.

Besides discrete attributes, the concepts in Background Knowledge can contain attributes with continuous DoB distributions $p_A^c(a)$. For rating the specificity of such attributes, the differential entropy

$$h(A^c) := - \int_{\mathcal{D}_A} p_A^c(a) \cdot \log(p_A^c(a)) \, \mathrm{d}a,$$

can be employed as a continuous variant of entropy. However, differential entropy in some important properties differs from Shannon entropy, like being scale-dependent and possible taking negative values. Furthermore, when discretized, differential entropy does not converge to Shannon entropy in the limit. These properties are undesired, e.g. when rating ratio-scaled attributes, which can be given in different units of measurement, as well as making it difficult to calculate the overall complexity of a concept as the sum of its attribute specificities. To overcome these limitations, a quantization of continuous distributions can be employed, based on defining a least decirnalbe quantum (*LDQ*) of information for each attribute [BB12]. The LDQ of an attribute thereby characterizes the level of precision at which attribute values are to be distinguished. For a continuous attribute A^c, the quantized entropy $H(A^c, \Delta_A)$ for the LDQ Δ_A is calculated by first discretizing the domain of A^c into bins of size Δ_A and assigning each bin the probability mass portion of $p_A^c(a)$ located within its extent. As result, a discrete attribute A^Δ with distribution $p_{A^\Delta}^d(a)$ is obtained, which in turn can be used as a basis for calculating Shannon entropy to rate the quantized entropy $H(A^c, \Delta_A) := H(A^\Delta)$ of the continuous attribute A^c. For rating the specificity of continuous attributes, limits for the attribute domain have to be given in order to calculate the number of bins resulting from the discretization of the attribute domain $\mathcal{D}_A$.

3.3 A Measure for Model Correspondence

Besides the complexity of OOWM Background Knowledge, the correspondence $L(\mathcal{R}|\mathcal{C})$ of modeled concepts $\mathcal{C}$ and so far observed information, stored as representatives $\mathcal{R}$ in the World Model, forms the second part of the proposed MDL-based quality measure. This correspondence reflects the fact that the better observed information can be explained by modeled concepts, the less description effort is necessary to store observation information. Therefore, the correspondence rating depicts the necessary description length. If a representative R matches a concept class C in Background Knowledge, it can be described through this concept. If not, it has to be described by using the best matching concept and, in addition, its differences to the concept. An appropriate correspondence measure can thus be given by

$$L(\mathcal{R}|\mathcal{C}) := \sum_{R \in \mathcal{R}} \sum_{C \in \mathcal{C}} p(C|R) \cdot L(R|C) \ ,$$

which calculates the expected overall correspondence based on the matching of all currently stored representatives R with all concepts C, weighted by their association probability $p(C|R)$. The matching $L(R|C)$ can be rated based on the attributes of a representative R according to

$$L(R|C) = \sum_{A_r \in \mathcal{A}_R} w_{A_{c_r}} \cdot L(A_r|A_{c_r}) \text{ with } A_{c_r} = \bar{A}(A_r) \in \mathcal{A}_C$$

being the concept attribute corresponding to the observed attribute A_r, and $w_{A_{c_r}}$ denoting a weighting factor that can differ for individual attributes. For grounding this approach, a measure for the description quality $L(A_r|A_{c_r})$ of a concept attribute A_{c_r} for an observation attribute A_r must be specified. In the MDL-approach taken, this measure should reflect how much additional information is necessary for representing the observed attribute on the basis of the concept attribute. For example, a deterministic observation value could be regarded as well represented if it lies within the bulk mass of a concept distribution. If it does not, its distance, e.g. to the mean, could be used to quantify the amount of additional description needed for representing the attribute. In case of the OOWM, where attribute values as described stochastically by DoB distributions, the attribute correspondence $L(A_r|A_{c_r})$ must constitute a function suitable for comparing probability distributions. If, in addition, LDQ quantization as presented above is employed, only discrete DoB distributions $p_A^d(a)$ have to compared. For this purpose, information-theoretic measures like the Kullback Leibler divergence

$$D_{KL}(A_r||A_{c_r}) = \sum_{a \in A_r} p_{A_r}^d(a) \cdot \log \left(\frac{p_{A_r}^d(a)}{p_{A_c}^d(a)} \right)$$

as well as cross entropy

$$H(A_r, A_{c_r}) = - \sum_{a \in A_r} p_{A_r}^d(a) \cdot \log \left(p_{A_c}^d(a) \right)$$

can be employed. In addition, the probabilistic versions (e.g. [Cha07]) of the distance measures presented in Section 2 can be applied as well as a discrete overlap measure

$$L_o(A_r, A_{c_r}) = \sum_{a \in A_r} l_o(a) \leq 1$$

using a value-based comparison of DoB distributions according to

$$l_o(a) := \begin{cases} 0, & \text{if } p^d_{A_r}(a) \leq p^d_{A_c}(a) \\ \left| p^d_{A_r}(a) - p^d_{A_c}(a) \right|, & \text{otherwise} . \end{cases}$$

For attribute correspondence, a measure should ideally assign a value close to zero to each observed attribute which is largely located within the bulk probability mass of its corresponding concept attribute. In turn, the assigned value should be the higher, the more apart the two probability masses lie.

4 Conclusion

This technical report proposes a conceptual approach to adaptive open-world modeling, which allows a world model like the OOWM to extend its a priori modeled Background Knowledge as needed for representing information on observed real-world objects. When applied in practice, the OOWM is likely to encounter entities during operation which cannot be represented by a necessary limited, a priori designed Background Knowledge. To cope with this limitation, an adaptive approach able to manage the knowledge for representing an application domain is needed. This approach has to adjust and extend Background Knowledge in accordance with the entities the OOWM has observed so far. As the basis of such an adaptive approach, the OOWM must be able to judge and evaluate how well suited its current Background Knowledge is for representing all observed real-world entities. A framework for evaluating model quality of Background Knowledge based on the Minimum Description Length principle was presented in this report. In this framework, model evaluation is based on quantitatively comparing attributes of entities and concepts. Related work concerning numerically evaluating the similarity of entities as well as the construction of entity hierarchies based on their similarity was presented.

Future work will concern an evaluation and a proof of concept for the presented framework by means of suitable examples. First results will be published in [KB13]. In addition, conceptions for the tasks of adjusting and extending existing concept classes have to be established as well as an approach to managing the hierarchy of concepts.

Bibliography

[BB12]   Andrey Belkin and Jürgen Beyerer. Information Entropy and Structural Metrics Based Estimation of Situations as a Basis for Situation Awareness and Decision Support. In *Proceedings of the IEEE Conference on Cognitive Methods in Situation Awareness and Decision Support*, New Orleans, USA, March 2012.

[BKFB12b]   Andrey Belkin, Achim Kuwertz, Yvonne Fischer, and Jürgen Beyerer. World Modeling for Autonomous Systems. In Christos Kalloniatis, editor, *Innovative Information Systems Modelling Techniques*. InTech, 2012.

[Cha07]   Sung-Hyuk Cha. Comprehensive Survey on Distance/Similarity Measures between Probability Density Functions. *International Journal of Mathematical Models and Methods in Applied Sciences*, 1(4):300–307, 2007.

[FB10b]   Yvonne Fischer and Alexander Bauer. Object-Oriented Sensor Data Fusion for Wide Maritime Surveillance. In *Proceedings of 2nd NURC International WaterSide Security Conference*, 2010.

[GHB08b]   Ioana Gheta, Michael Heizmann, and Jürgen Beyerer. Object Oriented Environment Model for Autonomous Systems. In Henrik Boström, Ronnie Johansson, and Joeri van Laere, editors, *Proceedings of the second Skövde Workshop on Information Fusion Topics*, pages 9–12. Skövde Studies in Informatics, 2008.

[Grü07]   Peter D. Grünwald. *The Minimum Description Length Principle*. The MIT Press, June 2007.

[HTF09]   Trevor Hastie, Robert Tibshirani, and Jerome Friedman. *The Elements of Statistical Learning: Data Mining, Inference and Prediction*. Springer, 2 edition, 2009.

[KB13]   Achim Kuwertz and Jürgen Beyerer. On Adaptive Knowledge Management for World Modeling. In *Proceedings of the IEEE Conference on Cognitive Methods in Situation Awareness and Decision Support*, 2013. Accepted for publication.

[Maq03]   Onaiza Maqbool. *Architecture Recovery of Legacy Software Systems Using Unsupervised Machine Learning Techniques*. PhD thesis, Lahore University of Management Science, 2003.

[Mit79]   Tom M. Mitchell. *Version Spaces: An Approach to Concept Learning*. PhD thesis, Stanford, CA, USA, 1979.

[Mit97]   Tom M. Mitchell. *Machine Learning*. McGraw-Hill Education (ISE Editions), 1st edition, October 1997.

[MS57]   Charles D. Michener and Robert. R Sokal. A Quantitative Approach to a Problem of Classification. *Evolution*, 11:490–499, 1957.

[PAM01]   K. Pedersen, J. K. Allen, and F. Mistree. Numerical Taxonomy: A Systematic Approach to Identifying Potential Product Platforms. In *Proceedings on the International Conference on Engineering Design (ICED'01)*, pages 515–522. WDK Publications, 2001.

[RS65]   F. James Rohlf and Robert R. Sokal. Coefficients of Correlation and Distance in Numerical Taxonomy. 45:3 — 27, 1965.

[Sch78]   Gideon Schwarz. Estimating the Dimension of a Model. *The Annals of Statistics*, 6(2):461–464, 1978.

[SM58]   Robert R. Sokal and Charles D. Michener. A Statistical Method for Evaluating Systematic Relationships. *University of Kansas Science Bulletin*, 38:1409–1438, 1958.

[Sok66]   Robert R. Sokal. Numerical Taxonomy. *Scientific American*, 215(6):106 — 116, 1966.

Challenges of Position Coding with Thermal Patterns

Sebastian Höfer

Vision and Fusion Laboratory
Institute for Anthropomatics
Karlsruhe Institute of Technology (KIT), Germany
sebastian.hoefer@kit.edu

Technical Report IES-2012-07

Abstract:
   Various surface inspection methods in computer vision rely on structured lighting techniques for position encoding. While these methods benefit from the rapid development in display technology and are well advanced in the visible spectrum, available technology is scarce outside the visible spectrum and narrows down to special applications. Choosing the right part of the spectrum for a computer vision task is a system design parameter which allows to emphasize or suppress specific optical properties of a material.
   This technical report will highlight the challenges of applying structured lighting techniques to the thermal infrared spectrum, which is primarily the creation of the appropriate patterns in this spectrum. Apart from the familiar effects in the visible spectrum, properties like self-emission, thermal diffusivity and differing optical characteristics have to be taken into consideration and demand for adaptations of the existing techniques.

1   Introduction

Inspection, measurement and reconstruction of surface geometries is one of the most important fields in computer vision. Besides techniques based on range sensors, triangulation by stereo vision is the most common method for determining a 3D-position. Triangulation in stereo vision requires a surface to be acquired by multiple cameras and to find corresponding points in the images to calculate their 3D-position. This requires a setup where the position of the cameras is calibrated beforehand. Difficulties arise if the surface under inspection doesn't show enough features, thus making it difficult to find correspondences between the camera images. Coded structured light techniques circumvent this problem by replacing one of the cameras with a projector which projects a code pattern on the surface. The code pattern or a sequence of patterns assigns each position in the projected image an unique code and enables for an easy way to identify a position in the camera images. All surfaces exhibiting an at least partial diffuse reflection can be inspected this way.

In contrast to the coded light techniques described above, the focus in this technical report is on applications of the deflectometric inspection method. Deflectometry is especially suitable for the inspection of specular surfaces. While it uses the same coding techniques as structured lighting, in deflectometry the patterns are not projected onto the surface. Instead the camera observes the reflection of these pattern on the surface under inspection. After decoding and evaluating the code patterns it is possible to reconstruct the inspected surface, if the geometry of camera and displayed pattern is calibrated beforehand and some preconditions are met [Wer11]. The reason to choose deflectometry to demonstrate the use of thermal patterns for position coding is the fact that the long wavelength thermal infrared spectrum is beneficial for the application in deflectometry, but we will elaborate on that in the next chapter.

We will start in the first chapter with characterizing the differing optical properties which come along with the long wavelength infrared spectrum and outline some essentials of infrared imaging. In the next chapter we will proceed to the constraints imposed by the spectrum and technology on the coded pattern generation and interpretation. We will conclude in chapter four.

2   Infrared Spectrum

Considering an application for deflectometric inspection there are two wavelength-dependent effects, which would favor the long wavelength of the thermal infrared spectrum. We will outline the nature and achievable benefits of these effects in the first section. Additionally, we will go into particulars about the differences in camera technology one has to bear in mind when implementing coded light techniques in the thermal infrared spectrum.

2.1   Benefits of longer wavelengths

First of all there are the wavelength-dependent differences in absorptivity, transmissivity, and reflectivity of materials themselves. While these effects are also

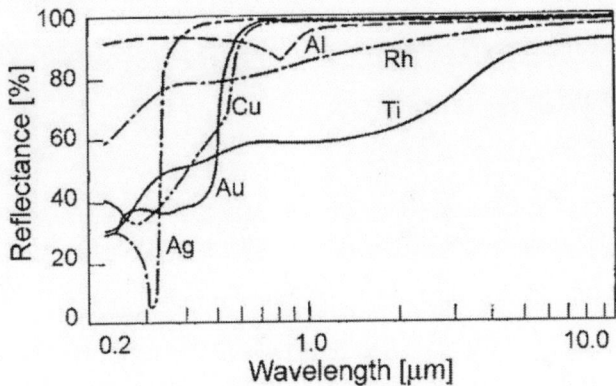

Figure 2.1: Reflectance of different metals as a function of wavelength. With increasing wavelength most metals become nearly fully reflective. (Source: [Dan10])

used in the visible spectrum for optimizing a machine vision process, the differences are a lot more distinctive in the thermal infrared spectrum due to the considerably higher wavelengths. This change in optical properties is most beneficial for metallic surfaces. Especially their reflectivity increases significantly for longer wavelength and whereas polished metals already exhibit good reflectivity in the visible spectrum they become nearly perfect mirrors in the thermal infrared spectrum [Dan10] (Fig. 2.1). A better reflectivity obviously benefits the deflectometric inspection and a lot of workpieces exhibit raw metal surfaces before finishing or lacquering.

Another interfering optical property for the deflectometric inspection is the transparency of a material. If on transparent materials the wanted reflection is overlaid by the background and multiple reflexions the decoding of the patterns can fail. In this case the use of the thermal infrared spectrum can be of use as well, since materials like glass or several transparent synthetic materials lose their transparent properties in this spectrum and become opaque 2.2. This effect, which can also be attributed to the wavelength-dependency of optical properties, enables transparent materials for deflectometric inspection.

Moreover, another effect leads to a further increase in reflectivity, as the scattering of light on rough surfaces is also wavelength-dependent. On a rough surface this effect is caused by its microstructure which is in the same order of magnitude as the wavelength of the light. The ratio between the amount of the specular reflection

(a)   (b)

Figure 2.2: Images of a glass lens in the visible light spectrum between $400 - 700\ nm$ (a) and in the thermal infrared spectrum between $8 - 14\ \mu m$ (b). In the visible spectrum the stripe pattern in the background is seen multiple times because of internal reflections, while the thermal spectrum shows only the reflection on the surface.

R compared to the amount R_0 at a perfectly smooth surface can be described by:

$$\frac{R}{R_0} = e^{-(4\pi\sigma)^2/\lambda^2} + c\frac{\sigma^4}{\lambda^4}, \tag{2.1}$$

where σ denotes the mean square roughness of the surface, λ the wavelength of the incident light and c is a constant dependent on the surface inclination and angle of acceptance of the measuring sensor [BP61, HK05]. This indicates a significant increase in reflectivity for longer wavelengths. Figure 2.3 illustrates this effect by plotting the ratio R/R_0 as a function of the surfaces mean square roughness σ using a simplified version of Eq.(2.1), where the influence of sensor characteristic and surface inclination is omitted:

$$\frac{R}{R_0} = e^{-(4\pi\sigma)^2/\lambda^2}.$$

It is shown that by using light of the far infrared spectrum $(8 - 14\mu m)$ one can obtain a specular reflection on surfaces with a mean square roughness one magnitude higher as it would be possible in the visible spectrum. This range of surface roughness comes within the limits exhibited by many machined materials, which makes the application of thermal infrared deflectometry viable for materials in early production stages.

All in all enables the thermal infrared spectrum the deflectometric inspection of many materials which are difficult to inspect in the visible spectrum, if at all

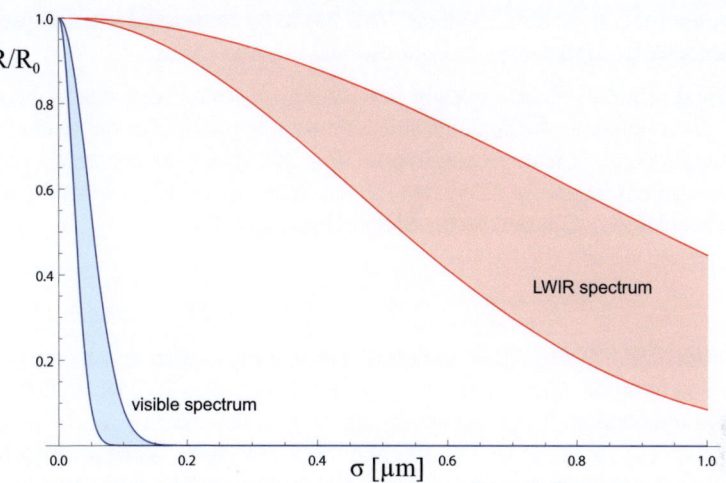

Figure 2.3: Ratio of the reflectances R/R_0 as a function of σ, the mean square roughness of the surface. The blue plot stands for the visible spectrum and the red plot for the LWIR spectrum ($8 - 14\mu m$). The longer wavelength shows a significant increase in reflectivity for the same surface roughness.

possible. A drawback of the longer wavelength is a loss in resolution when resolving small structures. But this limitation is of no consequence considering the low resolution of thermal infrared cameras compared with cameras for the visible spectrum.

2.2 Cameras for the long wavelength infrared spectrum

The thermal infrared spectrum can be divided into three spectral bands, whose boundaries are defined by atmospheric windows. Only in these bands is the atmospheric absorption low enough to allow infrared radiation to pass. There is the NIR band, adjacent to the visible spectrum, the MWIR band from $3-5\mu m$ and the LWIR band from $8 - 14\mu m$. As there is no broadband sensor technology which covers all spectral bands at once, a camera with a specific sensor for each band is necessary [Bud10, Dan10]. The most common camera technology are systems based on microbolometers. These are basically sensors with single thermistor-based pixels and are generally less expensive and easier to handle as comparable sensor technologies. A drawback of microbolometer sensors is their fixed integration time due to their design, so the length of exposure can not be adjusted as it is common for conventional cameras. This has to be considered when implementing systems with coded patterns for the thermal infrared spectrum.

Thermal infrared cameras usually provide a gray-scale-image where the intensity of a pixel indicates the apparent temperature integrated over the field of view of the single pixel. It is important to note, that this is only an apparent temperature, as the camera internally calculates the real temperature T_{true} from the measured exitance M_{maesured} based on the Stefan-Boltzmann law:

$$M_{\text{maesured}} = \sigma T_{\text{rad}}^4 = \epsilon \sigma T_{\text{true}}^4 \Rightarrow T_{\text{true}}^4 = \frac{T_{\text{rad}}}{\sqrt[4]{\epsilon}},$$

with the Stefan-Boltzmann-constant σ. For that the emissivity ϵ has to be known, as the camera can only observe the apparent temperature T_{rad} which is the product of real temperature T_{true} and emissivity ϵ. This dependency can be exploited to create specific gray values in a thermal infrared image. While keeping a pattern at a constant temperature, the apparent temperature can be modulated by creating patterns from materials with different emissivity. Another method is to use the spatial coverage with emissive material for modulating the apparent temperature. As a single camera pixel integrates over structures below its resolution, a fine grained structured pattern below this resolution can be used to achieve this effect. This effect is known as dithering and for example used for gray-scale-images in newspapers where only one color is used for the print.

3   Pattern Codification

Conventional code patterns can be defined as two-dimensional images with a certain structure so that a set of pixels are easily distinguishable by means of a local coding strategy. There are numerous of these coding strategies with different approaches to enable a unique identification of positions in a pattern. A comprehensive survey is given in [SPB04]. They also establish a categorization of all strategies into three basic classes based on the way the code is build (Fig. 3.1):

- Direct coding,
- Spatial neighborhood,
- Time-multiplexing.

We will pick up on this categorization and go into detail on each category, the differences between them and their usability for the thermal infrared spectrum.

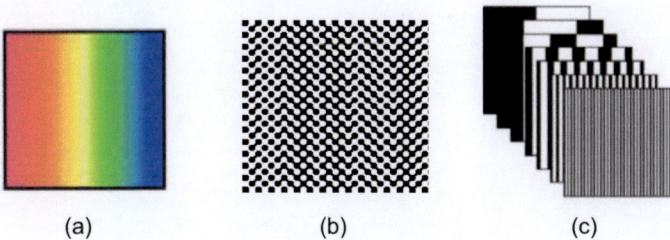

(a) (b) (c)

Figure 3.1: Examples for different categories of coding techniques: (a) color pattern for direct coding of the position, (b) resulting pattern of a De Bruijn graph, (c) binary pattern sequence of a time-multiplexing method (Source: [SPB04]).

Direct coding describes coding techniques, where the entire information for a unique identification of a pixel[1] is represented in it. In the visible spectrum this is usually realized by encoding employing color or gray values. Its advantage is its simplicity, which allows to capture the whole code with a single image. But its disadvantages often prevent its practical application. First of all the color or gray value observed by the camera also depends on the color of the surface where it is reflected or projected on. To compensate for the influence of the surface, a reference image is necessary, which diminishes the advantage to capture the code in a single image. Moreover, the distinction of color or gray values is very sensitive to noise, what further narrows its usability.

Considering the use of direct coding for the thermal spectrum, one at first misses the availability of *colors* for this spectrum. Colors would have to be especially compounded from materials which exhibit a distinctive characteristic for each of the infrared spectral bands. Furthermore, multi-spectral cameras for the thermal infrared are scarce and considerably more expensive compared with cameras for a single spectral band. Hence, color coding in thermal infrared spectrum is, despite being possible, no attractive option. Using gray values for encoding is in comparison a lot more viable encoding strategy. Patterns can be printed with a material with high thermal emissivity onto a support material with low emissivity, e.g. copper. Different gray values can be realized via dithering, thus an apparent gray value can be modulated by the ratio of emissive to non-emissive surface area. If the dithering-pattern is small compared to the cameras resolution, a homogeneous distribution of gray values can be achieved this way (Fig. 3.2). But even if an application realizes direct coding in the thermal spectrum via gray-values

---

[1]We will consistently use the term *pixel* for a display point, even though most thermal display technologies do not have quantized image points as monitors or projectors do.

(a)   (b)

Figure 3.2: Examples for a static code pattern for the thermal infrared spectrum on a printed copper board (a). The imprinted color reveals its temperature due to its high emissivity, while the bare copper exhibit near zero emissivity. By modulating the ratio of areas with high and low emissivity by the use of dithering, even gray values can be produced in the thermal image (b) while the whole pattern has actually the same temperature.

or *colors*, it still has to face the intrinsic disadvantages of this coding technique: noise-sensitivity and dependency on the spectral surface characteristics.

Spatial neighborhood   categorizes all encoding techniques which use a single unique pattern for encoding. The codeword for each pixel is contained in the neighborhood of its surrounding pixels and the features usually consist of their intensity and color. Every possible combination of surroundings for a pixel occurs only once in the pattern, thus every position can be uniquely identified. As these methods require a certain amount of pixels to compose a neighborhood, they trade off lateral resolution against speed. For the lower resolution they gain the possibility to capture the code in a single image. However, difficulties arise if the neighborhood cannot be identified. Especially in an application in deflectometry the code patterns often get heavily distorted, depending on the curvature of the surface under test. Such scaling, inverting and distortion of the pattern results in decoding errors if the algorithm does not fail completely.

If we take into account the use of spatial neighborhood methods in the thermal infrared spectrum, the use of a single static code pattern is particularly beneficial. As for the direct coding technique, the same restrictions to the use of color apply. Therefore, spacial neighborhood methods with static gray oder binary patterns are well-suited for the application in thermal infrared spectrum. But considering an application for deflectometric inspection, spatial neighborhood methods are intrinsically unsuited due to their susceptibility to pattern distortions, despite their general suitability for realizing thermal code patterns. Moreover, it is less attractive to sacrifice lateral resolution for the coding method when using thermal cameras, as the available sensor resolutions are way below the resolutions available for cameras in the visible spectrum.

Time-multiplexing is the last and most common category of encoding techniques. Techniques of this category distribute the code over a series of images, which are successively displayed or projected. In this way they trade off the time necessary to capture a whole code sequence for a high accuracy and robustness. As each pixel obtains its own code, the full resolution of the display can be used and there are usually no dependencies between neighboring pixels. Therefore, time-multiplexing techniques are, up to a certain degree, resistant towards distortions of their code patterns. Commonly used codes are binary codes (e.g. Gray-codes) phase-shift-codes and their combinations. For deflectometric inspections phase-shift-codes have become prevalent. They have the advantage to be insusceptible towards blurring of the code pattern, which is significant in deflectometry, as the camera is mostly focused onto the surface under inspection and the pattern in the reflection is out of focus. As the name already implies, phase-shift-codes evaluate the phase signal of a pattern sequence. The most common method is to use a sinusoidal pattern shifted multiple times and calculate the position of each pixel in this pattern by the intensity values captured for the pixel [Wer11]. Following this, the ambiguity of the phase signal has to be resolved, as the sine pattern repeats itself and therefore offers multiple solutions for the positions. This is usually done by capturing a second phase-shift-sequence with a different wavelength for the pattern and, what is more, the whole procedure has to be repeated horizontally and vertically as the pattern only encodes one dimension.

Despite their good suitability for the deflectometric inspection, is it challenging to implement time-multiplexing codes for the thermal infrared spectrum. A single static image of the pattern, which are mostly binary or gray-value images, can easily produced with techniques described above. But to produce a complete sequence the pattern has to be exchanged, which requires a complex mechanical mechanism, or has to be created dynamically by an thermal display. The main challenge in creating a dynamic display is the controlled transfer of heat to create specific patterns. There is no technology like displays or LEDs for the thermal infrared spectrum, which can instantly be switched on and off and available micro-mirror-technology is not applicable to wavelength far beyond the visible spectrum. The only available projector technology is military test equipment and not available for civil uses.

4 Conclusion

This technical report has given a brief overview over the benefits, which motivate the application of deflectometry to the thermal infrared spectrum. From this application arises the question, what position coding techniques are best suited for this task. An assessment of the practicability for the implementation of the different techniques was given, while focusing on an application in thermal infrared deflectometry. In conclusion, the thermal infrared spectrum shows promising results for a inspection of materials yet unamenable to deflectometry, with time-multiplexing as the best suited coding technique. Nonetheless, the lack of available thermal display technology demands for further development in this area, before a practical implementation is possible.

Bibliography

[BP61]   H. E. Bennet and J. O. Porteus. Relation between roughness and specular reflectance at normal incidence. *Journal of the Optical Society of America*, 51(2):123–129, 1961.

[Bud10] Gerald Budzier, Helmut ; Gerlach. *Thermische Infrarotsensoren : Grundlagen für Anwender*. Wiley-VCH, Weinheim, 2010.

[Dan10] Arnold Daniels. *Field Guide to Infrared Systems, Detectors, and FPAs*. The field guide series. SPIE Press, Bellingham, Washington USA, 2010.

[HK05]   Jan Horbach and Sören Kammel. Deflectometric inspection of diffuse surfaces in the far–infrared spectrum. In J. R. Price and F. Meriaudeau, editors, *Machine Vision Applications in Industrial Inspection XIII*, volume 5679 of *Society of Photo-Optical Instrumentation Engineers (SPIE) Conference Series*, pages 108–117, 2005.

[SPB04] Joaquim Salvi, Jordi Pagès, and Joan Batlle. Pattern codification strategies in structured light systems. *Pattern Recognition*, 37(4):827 – 849, 2004.

[Wer11] Stefan Bruno Werling. *Deflektometrie zur automatischen Sichtprüfung und Rekonstruktion spiegelnder Oberflächen*. Schriftenreihe Automatische Sichtprüfung und Bildverarbeitung. KIT Scientific Publishing, 2011.

Towards Gaze Analysis in Mobile Applications

Jan Hendrik Hammer

Vision and Fusion Laboratory
Institute for Anthropomatics
Karlsruhe Institute of Technology (KIT), Germany
jan.hammer@kit.edu

Technical Report IES-2012-08

Abstract:
   Gaze analysis gives us detailed information on the visual attention of a person. Further insights into the world of thought can be revealed and the information can contribute to interest or intention deduction. That is why eye tracking is extremely interesting for a variety of applications and different research fields. Especially due to the usage of mobile unobtrusive eye trackers, experimental setups can stay closer to reality and eye tracking becomes possible in settings where one didn't imagine it to be realisable years ago. But still, commercial off-the-shelf eye trackers do neither enable for 3D gaze point computation nor have solutions for fully automated gaze analysis in environments with real 3D objects. In this article we show which information mobile eye trackers need to deliver to make 3D gaze point computation on real 3D objects in known environments possible. We also demonstrate how this has been achieved for the Dikablis Wireless eye tracking system. We further show real time processing of 3D gaze points for fixation determination and an accuracy test to evaluate the developed algorithms.

1 Introduction

Gaze analysis is performed to find out about the visual attention of a user. Here the following questions are of interest: What are the visually most interesting objects in the scene? How often do special objects attract visual attention? In which order are objects looked at? How intensively is a certain area inspected? The answers to these questions make it possible to rearrange products in stores, change the layout of user interfaces or adverts, analyse how people look at pictures, when they are doing sports and analyse the gaze behaviour of people under stress in military applications. Due to the usage of mobile eye trackers, people are not restricted in their movements any more compared to settings with stationary eye trackers, where the head of the subject has to stay in some virtual head box to enable head tracking. With mobile eye trackers people can move around freely, since the eye tracker is worn as some type of glasses. This makes experimental setups more realistic and enables gaze not only for analysis purposes but also for implicit and explicit interaction in mobile applications or multi large-scale display environments where mice and keyboard are not suitable. There, implicit interaction takes place when the system observes a user freely viewing the environment. Gaze analysis is then used to assist the user for example by providing meaningful information on one of the displays. Furthermore eye tracking can be used for explicit interaction, e.g. when buttons appearing on a distant display can be selected by dwell time.

In this paper we describe what is necessary for realising fully automated gaze analysis in environments with 3D objects. We show in section 2.1 how the Dikablis Wireless eye tracking system has been used to compute 3D gaze points. Section 2.2 describes how a 3D scan path is analysed for eye movements and section 2.3 presents a methodology for evaluating algorithms for eye movement computation as well as results of a conducted accuracy test.

2 Gaze estimation in 3D environments

Gaze analysis generally consists of the following three sub-tasks:

- Eye tracking

- Gaze movement computation

- Fixation path analysis

First, the eye has to be tracked and the line-of-sight to be estimated. Gaze points on complex 3D objects can only be computed with the line-of-sight. Knowing the line-of-sight, its intersection with a 3D model of the environment results in the 3D gaze point. The sequence of gaze points is further analysed for eye movements, since raw gaze points do not necessarily refer to what a person is visually processing. Only during fixations the visual perception of the environment takes place. The eye movement path can then be analysed for visual attention using different metrics as proposed by Goldberg and Helfman [GH10]. The following sections will concentrate on gaze point and gaze movement computation in 3D environments.

2.1   The Dikablis Wireless eye tracking system

The Dikablis Wireless[1] is a monocular eye tracker using an active sensor with an infrared diode to observe the left eye of a person. Additionally a scene camera is attached to capture the scene in front of the test person. A picture of the Dikablis Wireless can be found in Figure 2.1(a). Both, scene and eye camera, can be rotated to adjust the eye tracker to different head shapes. Together with the eye tracker the person wears a battery and a sender clipped to a belt or worn in a waistcoat. The images of the scene and eye camera are transmitted wireless to the eye tracking notebook where they are processed. The eye tracking and a live tracking mechanism, which tracks markers attached to the scene, is performed. The latter allows the referencing of gaze data to the scene. This process is described in the next section.

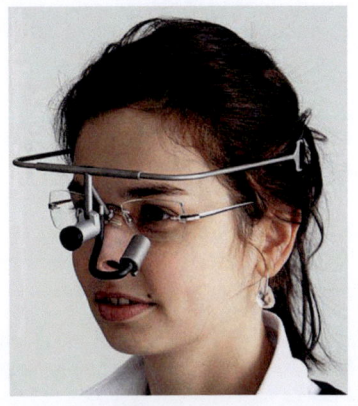 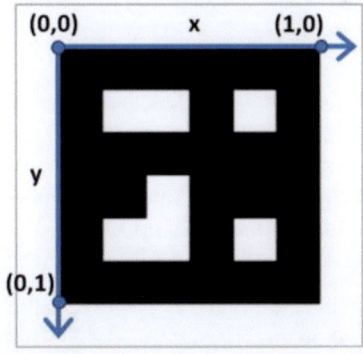

(a) Dikablis Wireless system   (b) Marker of Dikablis life tracking module

Figure 2.1: The Dikablis eye tracker and an example of a marker used for calibration and gaze computation with its virtual 2D plane.

2.1.1   Line-of-sight computation

The eye has different axes as can be seen in Figure 2.2. The optical axis is the line intersecting the centre of rotation of the eye, the nodal point of the eye and the pupil centre. The line-of-sight - or visual axis - is the line intersecting the centre of the fovea and the nodal point of the eye. The visual axis is the one of interest because its intersection with the environment results in the actual gaze point. For

---

[1]http://www.ergoneers.com/de/products/dlab-dikablis/overview.html

more information on how eye trackers can compute the line-of-sight, we refer to
Guestrin and Eizenman [GE06].

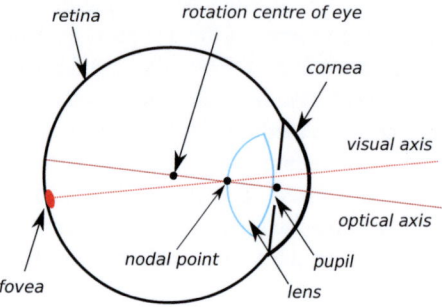

Figure 2.2: Structure of the human eye and visualisation of the optical and visual
axis.

Unfortunately the Dikablis Wireless eye tracking software and most other equiv-
alents from other companies do not provide the eye position and the line-of-sight
vector. However, the Dikablis software contains a live tracking module which de-
tects different markers in the images of the scene camera. One example of such
a marker can be found in Figure 2.1(b). Sixteen different types of markers are
available and can be placed anywhere in the environment.

Each of the markers spans a virtual 2D plane in the 3D space with an x- and y-
coordinate. For example the coordinates (1,0) describe the upper right corner of the
black square of the marker visualised in Figure 16, the coordinates (1,1) resemble
the lower right corner. The virtual 2D plane rotates with the marker. This means
the 6 degrees-of-freedom for the marker's virtual 2D plane are determined by the
marker's position and rotation in the 3D space. The live data sent over TCP/IP by
the eye tracking software contains the intersections of the line-of-sight, computed
by the Dikablis eye tracking software, with the virtual 2D plane of each marker
detected in the image of the scene camera. If a marker is attached to a wall, the
marker's virtual 2D plane coincides with the wall's surface and an intersection of
the line-of-sight with a marker's virtual plane can be interpreted as the gaze point.
If the scene is not only a wall but a complex 3D scene with objects whose surface
is different from a 2D plane, gaze computation using the Dikablis Wireless system
becomes more difficult. Assuming that the markers are distributed equally over
the scene somewhere between the objects, e.g. by using stands, and the position
and rotation of the markers is known, the intersections of the line-of-sight with
the detected marker's virtual planes can be used to reconstruct the line-of-sight.

Together with the calibration of the scene camera and an estimation of the eye position relative to the scene camera, one intersection is enough to compute the line-of-sight.

2.1.2 3D gaze point computation

For the computation of a gaze point at a special point of time the eye position, the direction vector of the line-of-sight and a 3D model of the environment must be available. We have manually created 3D models of different test environments and developed software for importing the well-known OBJ data format. This allows for having a 3D mesh of triangles which can be intersected with the line-of-sight. The intersection in viewing direction closest to the eye is the wanted gaze point. Knowing the information of the eye position, the line-of-sight and the gaze point, eye movements can be computed. This is described in the following section.

2.2 Eye movement computation

To understand the visual perception of a scene, the two most important eye movement types have to be considered: fixations and saccades. Fixations are the dwells during which the gaze almost remains still and saccades describe the ballistic, rapid eye movements between fixations. Visual perception of the environment is only occurring during fixations [Tob10], when the field of view is imaged on the retina by the optical system of the eye.

Scan paths of raw gaze points computed by the above described procedure do not necessarily refer to what a person was attending, because gaze points are also measured during saccades when no visual processing takes place. The process of human visual perception takes place during fixations, when the gaze almost remains still. This is why fixations are of much higher interest for attention detection than raw gaze points. The ballistic jumps between fixations called saccades also tell us something about the visual behaviour of a person. Since fixations and saccades are recommended measures for user monitoring and the basis of further gaze analysis, the next sections describe how we use two widely known algorithms for detecting fixations and saccades from 3D gaze data: Velocity-Threshold Identification (I-VT) and Dispersion-Threshold Identification (I-DT) [SG00].

2.2.1 Velocity-Threshold Identification (I-VT) in 3D

The I-VT is a fast and easily to implement algorithm. It is based on point-to-point velocities given in pixels/s or °/s. If 2D gaze positions are given, as provided by normal eye trackers, the velocity is the spatial distance from one pixel to the other multiplied by the frequency the eye tracker is delivering the data. When two consecutive 3D gaze points, a last one and an older one, and the position of the eye corresponding to the last gaze point are given, two visual axis from the eye to the two gaze points can be computed as well as the angle included by these lines. This angle multiplied by the frequency of the eye tracker results in the angular velocity. After the actual spatial or angular velocity has been computed, the I-VT uses a spatial threshold to compare this velocity to. If the actual velocity is greater than this threshold, the last gaze point is assigned to a saccade otherwise to a fixation. As long as points are assigned to a fixation the new fixation centre is computed as the mass value of the gaze points belonging to the fixation. Optionally the I-VT can be extended by a temporal threshold that describes the minimal duration for fixations which is according to Rötting [Röt01] or Goldberg and Schryver [GS95] around 100 ms. The advantage of using the 3D version of the I-VT is that its threshold is independent of the distance between eye and gaze points.

2.2.2 Dispersion-Threshold Identification (I-DT)

The computation of the I-DT is based on the computation of the span of a set of points. The necessary condition for a fixation is that the duration between the first and last gaze point of a considered set is greater than a minimal temporal threshold for fixations. This is the same condition as also described before for the I-VT. In Figure 2.3 you see the computation of the span for a rectangle. This rectangle is created as the bounding box of the considered 2D gaze points.

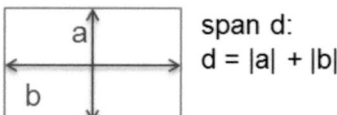

Figure 2.3: Computation of the span for I-DT.

The span is compared to a spatial threshold. If it is equal or smaller than the threshold, further gaze points are added to the set of considered gaze points. If it is greater, the temporal duration of the set is compared to the above described temporal threshold. If this duration is not smaller, the set of points is marked to be a fixation. The oldest gaze point is then removed from the set and the computation starts from the beginning.

When 3D gaze points are provided, the span is to be computed by angles between the visual axes to include the distance from the eye to the gaze points into the computation. Our adaption of the I-DT to its 3D version involves the creation of a plane E as visualised in Figure 2.4. Therefore the mass centre of all 3D gaze points $\mathbf{m}$ (green) is computed and used as point of support for E (grey). The vector from $\mathbf{m}$ to the eye $\mathbf{e}$, $\mathbf{e} - \mathbf{m}$, is used as normal for the plane E (red line), which can be defined, assuming the x-y-plane of the 3D world coordinate system is horizontal, by

$$E: \begin{pmatrix} x \\ y \\ z \end{pmatrix} = \mathbf{m} + s \cdot \mathbf{r_1} + t \cdot \mathbf{r_2}, \qquad x, y, z, s, t \in \mathbb{R}$$

with

$$\mathbf{r_1} \cdot (\mathbf{e} - \mathbf{m}) = 0$$
$$\mathbf{r_2} \cdot (\mathbf{e} - \mathbf{m}) = 0$$
$$\mathbf{r_1} \cdot (0, 0, 1)^T = 0$$
$$\mathbf{r_1} \cdot \mathbf{r_2} = 0$$

These equations ensure that $\mathbf{r_1}$ and $\mathbf{r_2}$ are orthogonal to each other, span E and $\mathbf{r_1}$ is parallel to the x-y-plane. Afterwards the lines from the eye to each gaze point are intersected with E and each intersection $\mathbf{b_i}$ (black) is transformed into the 2D coordinate system of E as shown in Figure 2.5, resulting in coordinates $\mathbf{b_1} = (s_1, t_1)^T, \ldots, \mathbf{b_B} = (s_B, t_B)^T$ with B being the number of intersections.

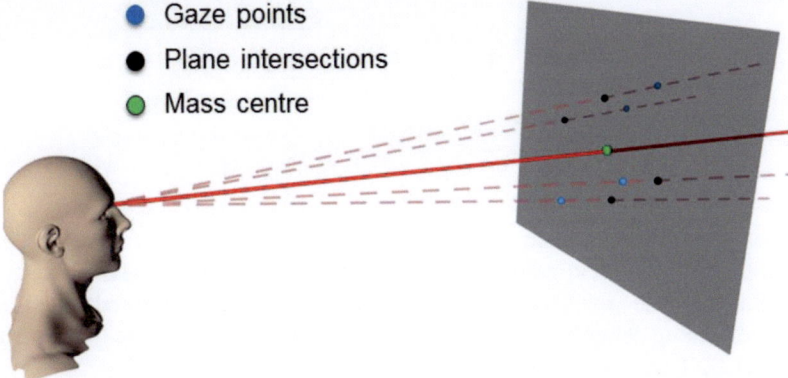

Figure 2.4: Visualisation of the construction of plane E.

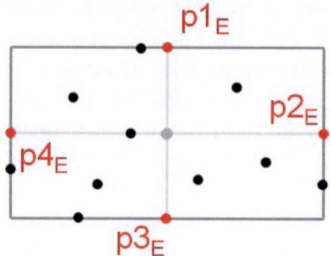

Figure 2.5: Visualisation of the intersections in plane E and of the resulting bounding box.

In the 2D coordinate system of E it is possible to compute the points $\mathbf{p1}_E$ to $\mathbf{p4}_E$ as follows:

$$\mathbf{p1}_E = ((x_1 + x_2)/2, y_2)^T$$
$$\mathbf{p2}_E = (x_2, (y_1 + y_2)/2)^T$$
$$\mathbf{p3}_E = ((x_1 + x_2)/2, y_1)^T$$
$$\mathbf{p4}_E = (x_1, (y_1 + y_2)/2)^T$$

with $0 < i \leq B$ and

$$x_1 := \min_i s_i, \quad x_2 := \max_i s_i, \quad y_1 := \min_i t_i, \quad y_2 := \max_i t_i.$$

The points $\mathbf{p1}_E$ to $\mathbf{p4}_E$ are then transformed back into the 3D space to yield the world points $\mathbf{p1}_W$ to $\mathbf{p4}_W$. The span d is computed with

$$d = \angle(\mathbf{p3}_W - \mathbf{e}, \mathbf{p1}_W - \mathbf{e}) + \angle(\mathbf{p2}_W - \mathbf{e}, \mathbf{p4}_W - \mathbf{e})$$

as the sum of the two angles between the vectors from the eye to $\mathbf{p3}_W$ and $\mathbf{p1}_W$ as well as to $\mathbf{p2}_W$ and $\mathbf{p4}_W$. By computing the span using angles, the threshold for the span becomes independent of the distance between eye and gaze points. The remaining computation of our 3D I-DT adaption is equivalent to the steps of the 2D I-DT version.

In the following section a methodology for evaluation eye movement algorithms is presented.

2.3   Methodology for gaze movement evaluation

In Komogortsev et al. [KJKG10] the authors describe a way for evaluating the accuracy of computed gaze movements. This procedure was also used to test the developed gaze movement computation algorithms and refine their parametrisation described in section 2.2. Therefore a tool for generating fixation stimuli was developed. It has the capability to show small coloured points on displays connected to a computer for a specified duration of time. Around ten test persons have been equipped with the eye tracker and instructed to look at the visualised points while the scan path was recorded. The positions of the visualised points can be used to compute ground-truth gaze points and these can afterwards be compared to the recorded scan path using different scores. An image of the scene can be seen in Figure 2.6(a). The shown frame was captured by the scene camera of the head mounted eye tracker. Detected markers (see section 2.1) are coloured with a bounding box and the gaze point projected into the image of the scene camera is visualised as a red dot. Close to the red dot a white dot can be seen. This white dot is the fixation stimulus - the point to be looked at. It can be seen that there is an offset between the red gaze point and the fixation stimulus. This is because the eye tracker was calibrated on the vertical monitor and the gaze overlay (red dot) computed by the eye tracker is only accurate in the calibration plane. In Figure 2.6(b) this is shown: The fixation stimulus is occluded by the visualised gaze point.

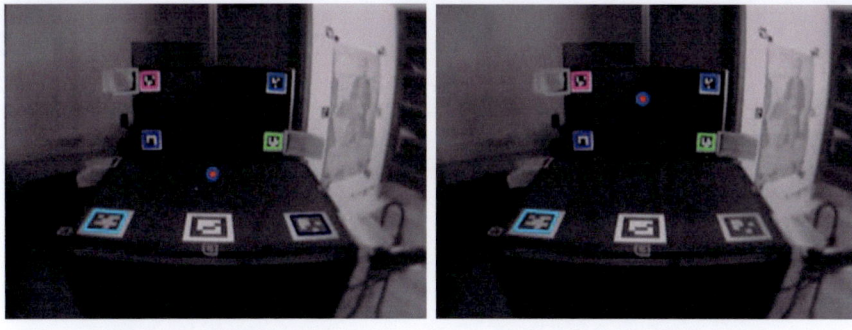

(a) Gaze on primary monitor   (b) Gaze on secondary monitor

Figure 2.6: Images of the scene camera overlaid with marker detections (squares) and gaze point (red).

2.3.1   Qualitative and quantitative scores

The scores used for evaluation are some of the scores developed by Komogortsev et al. [KJKG10]. Two important scores are the *Average number of fixations* (ANF) and the *Average fixation duration* (AFD). The ground truth for the ANF and AFD depends on the number of visualised fixation stimuli and the duration each stimulus was shown. Therefore the ground truth can be estimated. Two other important scores are the *Fixation quantitative score* (FQnS) and *Fixation qualitative score* (FQlS). The FQnS describes the percentage of time in which computed fixations are close to presented stimuli and is computed as follows:

$$ \text{FQnS} = \frac{\text{correct fixation gaze points}}{\text{total duration} \cdot \text{data rate}} $$

The *data rate* is the frequency the used eye tracker delivers data, e.g. with 60 Hz. The duration of a recorded scan path is the *total duration*. Gaze points assigned to computed fixations which are close to the corresponding stimuli are summed up in the *correct fixation gaze points*. Due to the definition a high FQnS is desirable. In reality an FQnS of 100 % is not possible because of the spatial difference of a visualised stimulus disappearing and reappearing at another position. The test person first has to realise this jump in the peripheral field of view, then has to compute a saccade to be able to fixate the new stimulus and then has to perform this saccade. This takes around 200 ms plus the saccade duration. According to Komogortsev et al. [KJKG10], where each stimulus was shown for 1.5 s, a FQnS > 70 % is considered to be a good result.

In comparison, the FQlS only takes into account the times when fixations are computed by the algorithm. Let $\mathbf{f}_i$ be the position of the i-th computed fixation with $0 \leq i \leq I$; J_i the number of single gaze points assigned to fixation i; $\mathbf{g}_{j_i,t}$ the position of a single gaze point computed at time t and having been assigned to fixation i as gaze point number j_i with $0 \leq j_i \leq J_i$; $\mathbf{s}_t$ be the position of the fixation stimulus shown at time t and $\mathbf{e}_t$ be the position of the eye at time t. The FQlS is then computed by:

$$ \text{FQlS} = \sum_{i=0}^{I} \sum_{j=0}^{J_i} \angle(\mathbf{f}_i - \mathbf{e}_t, \mathbf{s}_t - \mathbf{e}_t) $$

Hence, the FQlS describes the accuracy of the computed fixations. Due to this definition a low FQlS is desirable, why the best value for the FQlS would be 0°. This would mean that each classified fixation perfectly matched the presented stimulus.

A good fixation classification algorithm therefore should produce an FQnS above 70 % (when stimulus duration is 1500 ms) and a very low FQlS near to 0°. Evidently the last value also depends on the eye tracker itself and the quality of the calibration. The used eye tracker has an accuracy of around 0.5°. This means that with a good calibration, values of around 1.5°-2.5° would still be considered very good results.

2.4   Evaluation of experiments concerning fixation computation

In the following sections the evaluation of the previously described algorithms is presented. The I-VT in the original version and the version enhanced with the threshold for a minimal duration for fixations are tested with thresholds between 5°/s and 150°/s in steps of 5°/s. The third algorithm tested is the I-DT where thresholds between 0.02° and 1.94° in steps of 0.06° are chosen. To visualise the results, the ranges tested where mapped to the same scale by using range factors.

2.4.1   Average number of fixations (ANF)

15 points were shown for 1.5 s to 2.5 s during each experiment. It can further be assumed that the stimulus was earliest looked at 300 ms after it changed its position. Each point was fixated for about 1.2 s to 2.2 s. It is very likely that persons blinked during longer visualisation times for single points. Due to that some of the algorithms split one fixation into two or even more fixations although the same stimulus was looked at. Therefore the resulting number of fixations ranges between 15 and approx. 25 fixations. The results for the classification algorithms can be seen in Figure 2.7 where it is observable that both I-VT versions can compute an average number of fixations between 15 and 25 fixations. The I-DT algorithm computes too high values for the ANF.

2.4.2   Average fixation duration (AFD)

As described above the average duration a fixation stimulus was visualised for was around 2 s, but it was looked at in average for around 1.7 s. Again, when looking at Figure 2.8, it can be seen that both I-VT versions produce this value for a range factor between 17 and 19. The I-DT algorithm computes a lot of fixations as seen by the ANF. This is also observable for the AFD since very short fixations are computed.

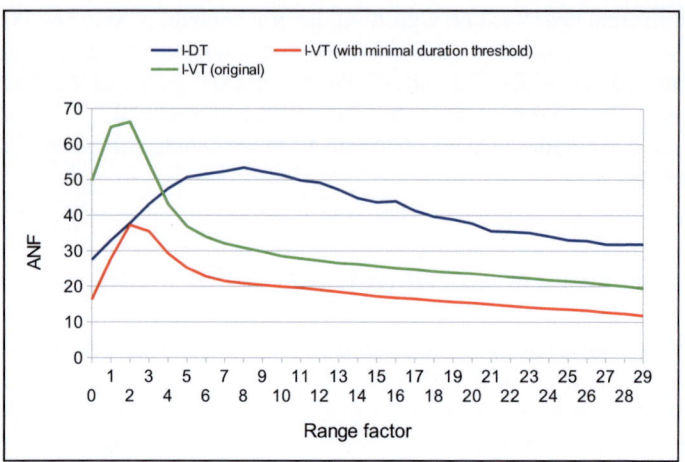

Figure 2.7: Results for the average number of fixations (ANF)

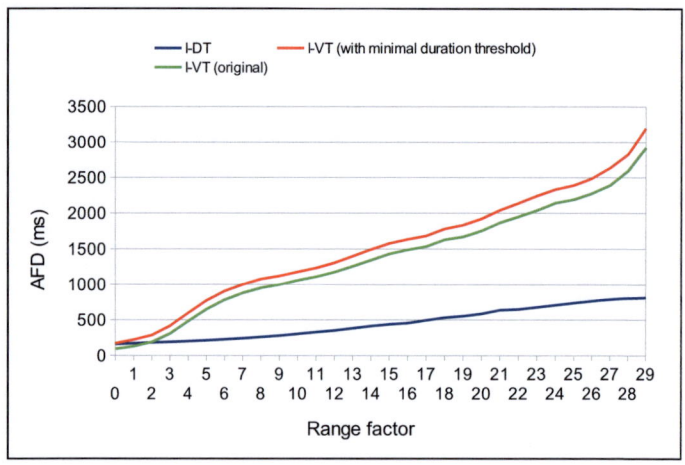

Figure 2.8: Results for the average fixation duration (AFD)

2.4.3   Fixation quantitative score (FQnS)

As visualised in Figure 2.9 the FQnS reaches a value of 70 % for both I-VT algorithms. Values above 85 % are practically not possible since we need around 300 ms to fixate a new stimulus point which were shown in average for around 2 s. Both I-VT versions reach a value of 70 %, which is considered as good in

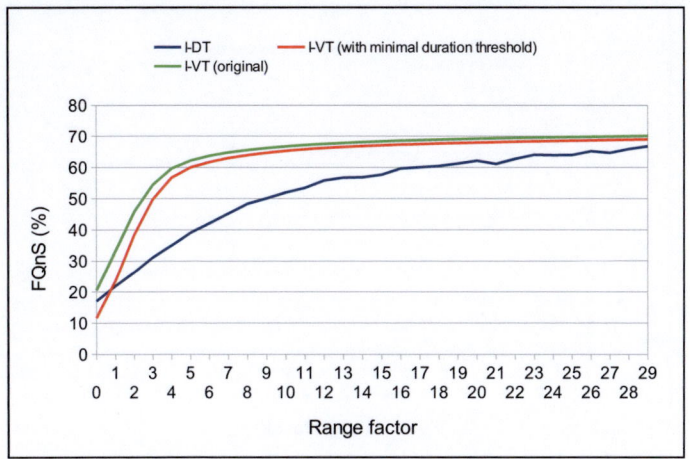

Figure 2.9: Results for the fixation quantitative score (FQnS)

[KJKG10]. The I-DT algorithm gets closer to 70 % for the higher range factors and might be getting even closer, but the range was limited for the evaluation. This is going to be repeated with higher scale factors in future evaluations.

2.4.4 Fixation qualitative score (FQlS)

The values for the FQlS given in Figure 2.10, all reside in between 3.4° and 4.3° which is not a good result concerning accuracy. This can be explained by several factors. First the live tracking of the markers and the online calibration are still work in progress and therefore were not used during the experiments. Hence the head position was nearly fixed during the experiments and the position of the left eye was measured. Since the heads of the participants could still slightly move the line-of-sight computation was not as accurate as if an online calibration using the detected markers would promise to be. Additionally the results were averaged over all participants and the eye tracking accuracy and calibration can be very different according to different persons due to worn glasses or make-up. Nevertheless, for some persons an average FQlS of 1.9° could be reached.

It can be concluded that the original I-VT and the slightly enhanced I-VT algorithms with thresholds mapped by range factors between 17 and 19 can be used for accurate fixation detection which is one of the most important issues for the detection of visual attention.

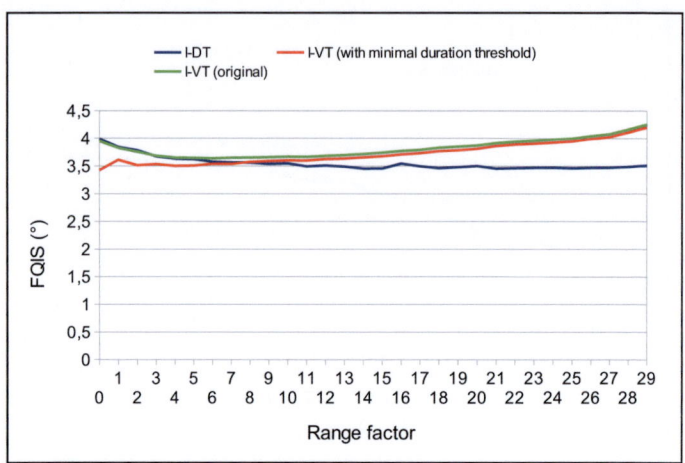

Figure 2.10: Results for the fixation qualitative (FQlS)

3   Conclusion

The more unobtrusive mobile eye trackers become, the more the demand for gaze analysis in different applications will grow. Gaze analysis will also be used in human-computer interaction to assist people when performing different tasks. Therefore it is necessary to provide a framework covering all the steps needed for automated gaze analysis in complex environments. In this article we have shown the steps that have to be performed and what data we need from eye trackers to realise fully automated gaze analysis. The presented adaptions of the fixation determination algorithms are real-time capable and show good accuracy under certain conditions with the used mobile eye tracker. Future work will concentrate on connecting different mobile eye trackers to the existing framework and realise important requirements of gaze analysis, e.g. 3D area-of-interest definition and gaze metric computation.

Bibliography

[GE06]   Elias Daniel D. Guestrin and Moshe Eizenman.   General theory of remote gaze estimation using the pupil center and corneal reflections. *IEEE transactions on bio-medical engineering*, 53(6):1124–1133, June 2006.

[GH10]   Joseph H Goldberg and Jonathan I Helfman. Comparing information graphics: A critical look at eye tracking. In *Proceedings of the 2010 Workshop on BEyond time and errors:*

novel evaLuation methods for Information Visualization, BELIV'10, pages 71–78, Atlanta, GA, USA, April 2010. ACM.

[GS95]   JosephH. Goldberg and JackC. Schryver. Eye-gaze-contingent control of the computer interface: Methodology and example for zoom detection. *Behavior Research Methods, Instruments, & Computers*, 27:338–350, 1995.

[KJKG10] Oleg V. Komogortsev, Sampath Jayarathna, Do Hyong Koh, and Sandeep Munikrishne Gowda. Qualitative and quantitative scoring and evaluation of the eye movement classification algorithms. In *Proceedings of the 2010 Symposium on Eye-Tracking Research & Applications*, ETRA '10, pages 65–68, New York, NY, USA, 2010. ACM.

[Röt01]   M. Rötting. *Parametersystematik der Augen- und Blickbewegungen für arbeitswissenschaftliche Untersuchungen*. Schriftenreihe Rationalisierung und Humanisierung. Shaker, 2001.

[SG00]   Dario D. Salvucci and Joseph H. Goldberg. Identifying fixations and saccades in eye-tracking protocols. In *ETRA '00: Proceedings of the 2000 symposium on Eye tracking research & applications*, pages 71–78, New York, NY, USA, 2000. ACM.

[Tob10]   Tobii Eye Tracking. An introduction to eye tracking and tobii eye trackers, January 2010.

Filter Optimization Approach for a Chromatic Confocal Triangulation Sensor

Miro Taphanel

Vision and Fusion Laboratory
Institute for Anthropomatics
Karlsruhe Institute of Technology (KIT), Germany
miro.taphanel@kit.edu

Technical Report IES-2012-09

Abstract:

Simplified, a chromatic confocal triangulation CCT sensor encodes different surface heights by different wavelengths. A height is measured by determining the corresponding wavelength of the optical signal. The CCT sensor concept solves this task using a multispectral camera, which is a camera with multiple channels, each characterized by a different optical filter. To measure the wavelength with high precision, these filters need to be optimized. For this purpose a physical model is introduced, which describes the multispectral camera. Based on this model, merit functions are developed that cover two aspects: increased resolution and statistical uniqueness of a measurement. These merit functions can be used in a next step to optimize a set of filters.

1 Introduction

This article is about how to optimize optical filters for a CCT sensor, which is a new type of 3D sensor [TB12]. Optimized optical filters play a key role in the CCT concept, because they mainly determine the measurement resolution. Figure 1.1 illustrates the principle optical setup of a CCT sensor. A polychromatic source is split up into monochromatic light, each wavelength focused on a different height. In combination with a surface, the optics assure that only light of the currently focused wavelength can reach the camera sensor (depicted as green light path). For this article this is an important detail, because the optical signal on the camera is known. The optical signal is assumed as a gaussian like shaped spectrum with a

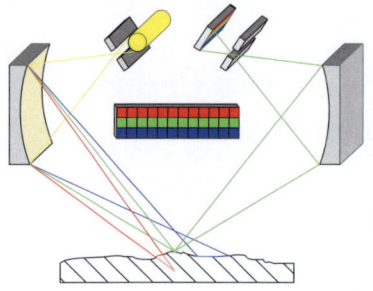 

Figure 1.1: On the right, prototype of a CCT sensor. On the left, principle optical setup of a CCT sensor with highlighted RGB line scan sensor. Important detail: Only the green illustrated wavelength can reach the RGB sensor.

FWHM[1] of a few nanometers. With this assumption, only the center wavelength is unknown and shifts according the current surface height respectively. This situation simplifies the task of the multichannel camera sensor, which is reduced to measure the center wavelength of the optical signal. The principle idea is depicted in Fig. 1.2. Each signal with defined center wavelength causes a unique color coordinate $g(\lambda_0)$. After an acquisition, the original surface height is deduced from the measured color coordinates. Optimal optical filters will be able to measure the center wavelength with high precision. The special feature of the proposed optimization approach is to optimize all optical filters simultaneously. A multispectral camera implicit span a multidimensional color space, which will be used to define optimality.

The abstract is organized as follows: In section 2 a physical model is derived that explains the camera acquisition process. In section 3 this model is used to define merit functions for optimization calculations. The optimization itself is not part of this report. Section 4 concludes with an outlook to future work.

2 Modeling of the Camera Sensor

2.1 Noiseless Forward Model

The objective of this section is to derive a mathematical model which explains a measured grey value vector $\mathbf{g} = (g_1, \ldots, g_n)^\top$ as a function of the optical signal

---

[1]Full width at half maximum

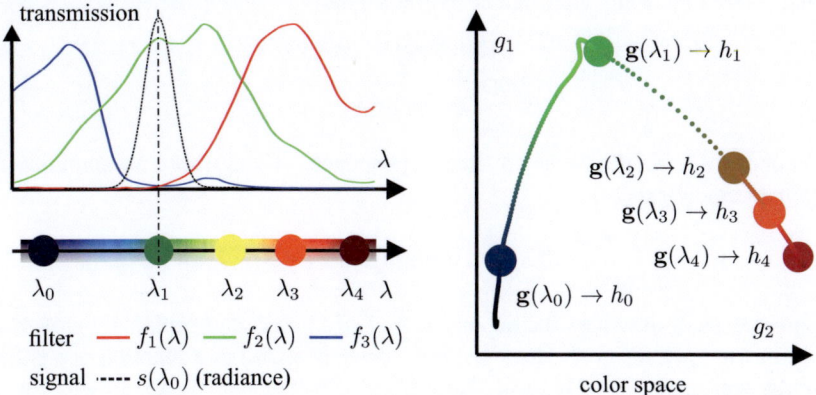

Figure 1.2: Measuring principle: A multichannel camera with optical filters (f_1, f_2, f_3) acquires a spectrum $s(\lambda_0, \lambda)$ which is centered around λ_0. Each center wavelength λ_0 causes a unique grey value vector $\mathbf{g}(\lambda_0)$ in color space. After an acquisition the center wavelength can be deduced from the color coordinate $\mathbf{g}(\lambda_0)$. (partly taken form [TB12])

$s(\lambda)$. The signal describes the spectral distribution of light $s(\lambda - \lambda_0)$, which is shifted towards a center wavelength λ_0 (cp. Fig. 1.2). According to the optical setup of the CCT sensor, this center wavelength λ_0 is directly related to a certain height.

The grey values of the multichannel camera are connected to four integrals which describe the image acquisition process of a camera without regard to noise:

$$\mathbf{g} \propto \int_T \int_A \int_\Lambda \int_\Omega q(\lambda)\mathbf{f}(\lambda, \mathbf{p}, \alpha)s(\lambda)\mathrm{d}\Omega\mathrm{d}\lambda\mathrm{d}A\mathrm{d}T. \qquad (2.1)$$

In detail an integration over the time T, the pixel area A, the wavelength range of the camera Λ, and the solid angle of the grating Ω. The filter vector $\mathbf{f}(\lambda, \mathbf{p}, \alpha) = (f_1, \ldots, f_n)^\top$ consists of optical transmission characteristics of each camera channel. These transmission properties depend on the wavelength λ, the incidence angle α, and a parameter vector $\mathbf{p}$. The parameter vector $\mathbf{p}$ determines the optical behavior of the filters and will be optimized later on (e.g. $\mathbf{p}$ describes the layer thicknesses of a thin film interference filter). The camera sensitivity or quantum efficiency $q(\lambda)$ has a spectral impact, too. Finally, the optical signal $s(\lambda)$ as radiance with spectral dependence is taken into account.

Using two assumptions, the model (2.1) can be simplified and extended. First of all, the solid angle describes a cone with a perpendicular main axis to the filters.

In this case, the solid angle can be expressed as:

$$\Omega = 2\pi(1 - \cos(\alpha))$$

$$\frac{\partial \Omega}{\partial \alpha} = 2\pi \sin(\alpha)$$

Second, all variables have no time dependence. Using these assumptions the camera model gets to:

$$\mathbf{g} \propto \int_{\Lambda} \left(\int_0^{\alpha_{\max}} \mathbf{f}(\lambda, \mathbf{p}, \alpha) 2\pi \sin(\alpha) \mathrm{d}\alpha \right) q(\lambda) s(\lambda) \mathrm{d}\lambda \, A_{\text{pixel}} T_{\text{int}}. \qquad (2.2)$$

Equation (2.2) describes the dependence of $\mathbf{g}(\lambda)$ on λ and explains a grey value vector for a given signal. However, the change of $\mathbf{g}(\lambda_0)$ as a function of a shifted center wavelength is of interest. An analytical model can be derived with the assumption, that the shape of the spectral distribution of $s(\lambda)$ keeps constant during a change of the central wavelength λ_0. Then the model can be expressed as:

$$\mathbf{g}(\lambda_0) \propto \int_{\Lambda} \left(\int_0^{\alpha_{\max}} \mathbf{f}(\lambda, \mathbf{p}, \alpha) 2\pi \sin(\alpha) \, \mathrm{d}\alpha \right) q(\lambda) s(\lambda - \lambda_0) \, \mathrm{d}\lambda$$

$$= \left(s(\lambda) * \int_0^{\alpha_{\max}} q(\lambda) \mathbf{f}(\lambda, \mathbf{p}, \alpha) 2\pi \sin(\alpha) \, \mathrm{d}\alpha \right) (\lambda_0), \qquad (2.3)$$

what is namely the noiseless forward model, which is used to explain the measuring process of the camera.

2.2 Analytical Derivation of the Noiseless Model

During optimization it is necessary to evaluate partial derivations of the merit function. In principle, this can be done numerically or analytically, in which analytical derivations lead to higher precision and faster computations [FT92]. For this reason, analytical derivations of the noiseless forward model (2.3) are performed in this section.

$$\frac{\partial \mathbf{g}(\lambda_0, \mathbf{p})}{\partial \lambda_0} = \left(\frac{\partial s(\lambda)}{\partial \lambda} * \left(q(\lambda) \int_{\Omega} \mathbf{f}(\lambda, \mathbf{p}, \alpha) 2\pi \sin(\alpha) \mathrm{d}\alpha \right) \right) (\lambda_0)$$

$$\frac{\partial \mathbf{g}(\lambda_0, \mathbf{p})}{\partial p_k} = \left(s(\lambda) * \frac{\partial}{\partial p_k} \left(q(\lambda) \int_{\Omega} \mathbf{f}(\lambda, \mathbf{p}, \alpha) 2\pi \sin(\alpha) \mathrm{d}\alpha \right) \right) (\lambda_0)$$

$$= \left(s(\lambda) * \left(q(\lambda) \int_{\Omega} \frac{\partial \mathbf{f}(\lambda, \mathbf{p}, \alpha)}{\partial p_k} 2\pi \sin(\alpha) \mathrm{d}\alpha \right) \right) (\lambda_0)$$

$$\frac{\partial^2 \mathbf{g}(\lambda_0, \mathbf{p})}{\partial \lambda_0 \partial p_k} = \left(\frac{\partial s(\lambda)}{\partial \lambda} * \left(q(\lambda) \int_{\Omega} \frac{\partial \mathbf{f}(\lambda, \mathbf{p}, \alpha)}{\partial p_k} 2\pi \sin(\alpha) \mathrm{d}\alpha \right) \right) (\lambda_0),$$

with parameter vector $\mathbf{p} = (p_1, \ldots, p_k, \ldots, p_m)$. The filter vector $\mathbf{f}(\mathbf{p}, \lambda, \alpha) = (f_1, \cdots, f_n)$ contains n filters and each filter can have an arbitrary number of parameters $p_k \in \mathbf{p}$. In the case of thin film filters, each parameter specifies a thickness of a thin film layer. The corresponding refractive index is given by the periodic change of high and low refractive indices. For thin film filters the analytical derivative $\frac{\partial f}{\partial p_k}$ can be further specified [LM08],[FT92].

Up to here, one aspect of the signal processing used in the CCT sensor was not discussed. A change of a grey value vector should indicate a change of λ_0. However, $\mathbf{g}$ will change due to changes in intensity of $s(\lambda)$, too (e.g. caused by changes in reflectance of the measured surface). To avoid this behavior, the grey value vectors are intensity normed by additional signal processing. Instead of measuring absolute values, relative grey values are used. An overview of possible algorithms can be found in [MJ12], however, the concrete implementation has no effect to the optimization process. In the same paper [MJ12] it is shown, that changes in

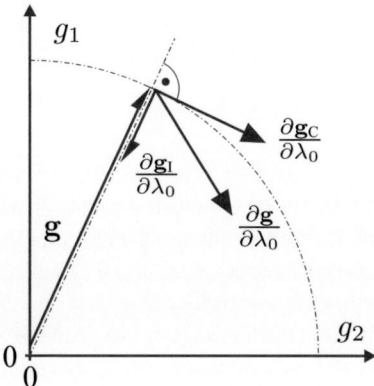

Figure 2.1: Vectorial decomposition of grey value changes caused by intensity and chromaticity changes. A detailed discussion can be found in [MJ12].

intensity are always towards the origin of the color space. This fact is used in the following to subtract vectorial changes of $\frac{\partial \mathbf{g}}{\partial \lambda_0}$ towards the origin. The result:

$$\frac{\partial \mathbf{g}_C(\lambda_0, \mathbf{p})}{\partial \lambda_0} = \frac{\partial \mathbf{g}(\lambda_0, \mathbf{p})}{\partial \lambda_0} - \frac{\partial \mathbf{g}_I(\lambda_0, \mathbf{p})}{\partial \lambda_0} \qquad (2.4)$$

$$= \frac{\partial \mathbf{g}}{\partial \lambda_0} - \frac{\left(\frac{\partial \mathbf{g}}{\partial \lambda_0}\right)^{\top} \mathbf{g}}{\mathbf{g}^{\top} \mathbf{g}} \mathbf{g},$$

is invariant to changes due to intensity changes. The index g_C indicates that only changes in *chromaticity* are of interest. The calculation of:

$$
\frac{\partial^2 g_C}{\partial \lambda_0 \partial p_k} = \frac{\partial^2 g}{\partial \lambda_0 \partial p_k} - \frac{\partial}{\partial p_k} \left(\frac{\left(\frac{\partial g}{\partial \lambda_0} \right)^{\top} g}{g^{\top} g} g \right)
$$

$$
= \frac{\partial^2 g}{\partial \lambda_0 \partial p_k} - \left(\frac{\left(\frac{\partial g}{\partial \lambda_0} \right)^{\top} g}{g^{\top} g} \right) \frac{\partial g}{\partial p_k}
$$

$$
- \left(\frac{\left(\left(\frac{\partial^2 g}{\partial \lambda_0 \partial p_k} \right)^{\top} g + \left(\frac{\partial g}{\partial \lambda_0} \right)^{\top} \frac{\partial g}{\partial p_k} \right) g^{\top} g \right) - \left(\left(\left(\frac{\partial g}{\partial \lambda_0} \right)^{\top} g \right) 2 \left(\frac{\partial g}{\partial p_k} \right)^{\top} g \right)}{(g^{\top} g)^2} \right) g
$$

is straight forward.

2.3   Noisy Extention of the Model

In this section the forward model (2.3) is extended in terms of noise. The idea to measure the wavelength λ_0 by its grey value vector $g(\lambda_0)$ requires implicit, that each central wavelength λ_0 has a unique grey value vector. This situation gets even worse, when g is modeled as random variable. To evaluate the uniqueness of two separate grey value vectors the probability of a false classification will be regarded in section 3.2. In high dimensional spaces the probability of false classification can either be approximated or calculated numerically[DHS01]. To avoid heavy numerical integrations an approximation is used. For this reason, a relatively rough noise model is sufficient, namely the assumption of normal like distributed noise. Fortunately, according to [JÖ5] all influences that contribute to noise in a camera can be regarded as normal like distributed.

$$
E\{g(\lambda_0)\} = g(\lambda_0)
$$

$$
\Sigma(g(\lambda_0)) = \begin{pmatrix} \sigma^2(g_1(\lambda_0)) & \cdots & 0 \\ \vdots & \ddots & \vdots \\ 0 & \cdots & \sigma^2(g_n(\lambda_0)) \end{pmatrix}
$$

$$
\text{with } g(\lambda_0) = (g_1(\lambda_0), \cdots, g_n(\lambda_0))^{\top}
$$

$$
\text{and } \sigma^2(g) = \sigma_{\text{dark}}^2 + K g(\lambda_0)
$$

Each camera channel is assumed as uncorrelated and the computation of the variance 2.3 is proposed in [JÖ5]. The factor K depends on the chosen camera.

3   Merit functions for Filter Optimization

An optimization process requires a merit function MF $: \mathbb{R}^m \rightarrow \mathbb{R}$ which defines optimality. During the optimization

$$\arg \min_{\mathbf{p}} \mathrm{MF},$$

the filter parameters $\mathbf{p} = (p_1, \ldots, p_m)^\top$ are adjusted to minimize MF, interpreted as costs. The optimality is defined in the multidimensional color space that is spanned implicitly by the multichannel camera, each channel featured by a separate optical filter. This approach allows to evaluate all filters simultaneously.

The purpose of optimization is to increase measurement resolution by optimized filters. However, this is constraint by the additional condition of unique mapping between a grey value vector $\mathbf{g}(h_0) \leftrightarrow h_0$ and the corresponding height. The merit function of section 3.1 can only be used to increase measurement resolution. In contrast, the merit function of section 3.2 only optimizes the uniqueness. Finally, in section 3.3 a merit function is proposed that covers both aspects simultaneously.

The CCT sensor is a 3D measurement system and the uncertainty of a measurement system is as high as its worst working point. That is why *minimax* optimization is of general interest, because the maximum costs, which define the sensor performance, need to be minimized. However, minimax optimization in thin film synthesis is avoided due to the complicated way of optimization [FT92] (p.106). Alternatively, the maximum operator can be approximated using the infinite *p-norm*:

$$\max_{i=1,\ldots,l} |\mathrm{MF}_i| = \lim_{p \to \infty} \|\mathbf{MF}\|_p = \lim_{p \to \infty} \left(\sum_{i=1}^{l} |\mathrm{MF}_i|^p \right)^{\frac{1}{p}}$$

This dependence is used with slight changes. First of all, the finite sum is replaced by an integral and the exponent $\frac{1}{p}$ is neglected because it is only scaling the result of the sum. In praxis, the infinity limes of p will be set to quite low values. Due to fast increasing behavior of exponential functions, this is a sufficient approximation:

$$\min_{\mathbf{p}} \max_{\lambda_0} \mathrm{MF} \approx \min_{\mathbf{p}} \int_{\lambda_{\min}}^{\lambda_{\max}} \mathrm{MF}(\mathbf{p}, \lambda_0)^q \, d\lambda_0, \text{ with } 0 < q \ll \infty$$

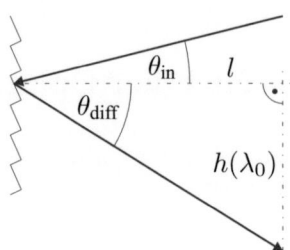

Figure 3.1: Relationship between height $h(\lambda_0)$ and center wavelength λ_0 using the grating equation.

This approximation of the maximum operator has the advantage, that the merit function is differentiable [FT92] (p. 107).

Another CCT senor specific aspect must be taken into account. The relation between measured height h_0 and center wavelength of the signal λ_0 is nonlinear (cp. Fig. 3.1). A weighting function $w(\lambda_0)$ is necessary to increase the costs for wavelengths that are encoding the height with less vertical resolution. This function is obtained according to the following considerations:

$$\mathbf{g}(h_0) = \mathbf{g}(\lambda_0(h_0))$$
$$\frac{\partial \mathbf{g}}{\partial h_0} = \frac{\partial \mathbf{g}}{\partial \lambda_0} \frac{\partial \lambda_0}{\partial h_0} = \frac{\partial \mathbf{g}}{\partial \lambda_0} \left(\frac{\partial h_0}{\partial \lambda_0} \right)^{-1}.$$

To express everything as a function of λ_0 is beneficial, because the previous results of section 2 can directly be reused. The relationship of $h_0(\lambda_0)$ can be obtained by using the grating equation [Loe97]:

$$\sin \theta_{\text{diff}} = \sin \theta_{\text{in}} + m\frac{\lambda}{d}, \text{ with } m = 0, \pm 1, \pm 2, \dots ,$$

with incident angle θ_{in}, diffracted angle θ_{diff}, order of diffraction m, and grating period d. According to a geometric setup of figure 3.1, the relationship between height $h_0(\lambda_0)$ and center wavelength λ_0 is given by:

$$h(\lambda_0) = l \tan \left(\arcsin \left(\sin \theta_{\text{in}} + m\frac{\lambda_0}{d} \right) \right),$$

with a distance l (grating surface to measurement plane). A change in wavelength causes a change in height according to:

$$\frac{\partial h(\lambda_0)}{\partial \lambda_0} = \frac{1}{\cos^2(\arcsin(\sin \theta_{\text{in}} + m\frac{\lambda_0}{d}))} \frac{1}{\sqrt{1 - (\sin \theta_{\text{in}} + m\frac{\lambda_0}{d})^2}} \frac{lm}{d},$$

where the fraction $\frac{lm}{d}$ can be neglected, because constant factors don't affect merit functions. Finally the following weight function is defined, which has high values in the case of a low sensitivity:

$$w(\lambda_0) = \cos^2\left(\arcsin\left(\sin \theta_{\text{in}} + m\frac{\lambda_0}{d}\right)\right) \sqrt{1 - \left(\sin \theta_{\text{in}} + m\frac{\lambda_0}{d}\right)^2}$$
$$\propto \left(\frac{\partial h(\lambda_0)}{\partial \lambda_0}\right)^{-1}$$

3.1 Merit Function to Rate Measurement Sensitivity

Measurement sensitivity in this section is defined as the change of the grey value vector due to a change in wavelength λ_0. According to figure 2.1, only changes are of interest, that are not caused by intensity changes. In this argumentation equation (2.4), as derivative of the chromaticity portion in color space, can directly be used:

$$\text{MF}_1 = -\min_{\lambda_0} \left\| w(\lambda_0)^{-1} \frac{\partial \mathbf{g}_C(\mathbf{p}, \lambda_0)}{\partial \lambda_0} \right\|_2^2. \tag{3.1}$$

The minimum operator takes into account, that only the worst case is optimized. In this case the working point λ_0 with lowest sensitivity. Because the worst case is indicated by minimal values, the weighting function $w(\lambda_0)$ is inverted and MF_1 is negative, to be maximized during optimization. Furthermore, an exponent of 2 is chosen which simplifies derivations of MF ($\|\mathbf{u}\|_2 = \sqrt{\mathbf{u}^\top \mathbf{u}}$ and $\|\mathbf{u}\|_2^2 = \mathbf{u}^\top \mathbf{u}$ which is easier to derivate). Finally, the euclidean norm $\|.\|_2$ is used to valuate all weighted partial derivations of $\mathbf{g}_C$.

Alternatively, without minimum operator, the merit function can be defined as:

$$\text{MF}_2 = \int_\Lambda \left\| w(\lambda_0)^{-1} \frac{\partial \mathbf{g}_C(\mathbf{p}, \lambda_0)}{\partial \lambda_0} \right\|_2^{-2q} d\lambda_0, \text{ with } 0 < q \ll \infty.$$

Consider the minus sign in the exponent, which is necessary to approximate the minimum operator of equation (3.1).

3.2   Merit Function to Rate Uniqueness

Each multidimensional color coordinate can encode a unique surface height and it is not allowed to assign two or more surface heights to one color coordinate $g(\lambda_0)$. This is even worse in respect of noise. Regarding two adjacent grey values g_i and g_j there will be made a false assignment with a certain probability P_{error}. The objective of this section is to derive a probability for false classification and use this expression to design a merit function. Optimization with such a merit function will reduce the probability of false classification. In Section 2.3 a noisy grey value vector was modeled as random variable with the assumption of a normal like distribution. This model can be used to calculate the probability $P_{\text{error}}(g_i, g_j)$. According to [DHS01] (p. 46) it is not possible to express this probability analytically. Instead, the use of an approximation of an upper bound, namely the *Chernoff Bound* or *Bhattacharyya Bound* is proposed. For our purpose the *Bhattacharyya Bound* is sufficient and most suited due to its analytical closed form. The upper bound of the false classification probability of two adjacent grey value vectors can be approximated by [DHS01]:

$$P_{\text{error}}(g_1, g_2) \leq \frac{1}{2}e^{-k} \text{ , with} \tag{3.2}$$

$$k = \frac{1}{8}(\mu_2 - \mu_1)^\top \left(\frac{\Sigma_1 + \Sigma_2}{2}\right)^{-1}(\mu_2 - \mu_1) + \frac{1}{2}\ln\frac{\det\left(\frac{\Sigma_1+\Sigma_2}{2}\right)}{\sqrt{\det\Sigma_1 + \det\Sigma_2}},$$

with the assumption of equal probabilities of occurrence $P(g_i) = P(g_j) = 0.5$.

To use equation (3.2) in a merit function it is necessary to establish a mechanism to rate an error probability with respect to the distance $\triangle\,\lambda = \lambda_j - \lambda_i$. It is obvious that adjacent grey value vectors ($\triangle\,\lambda \to 0$) will have a maximum possible error probability $P_{\text{error}}(g_i, g_j) = 0.5$. The easiest way to avoid this behavior is a distinction by cases:

$$P_{\text{error}}(g_1, g_2) \leq \begin{cases} \frac{1}{2}e^{-k} \\ 0 & \text{if } |\lambda_j - \lambda_i| < \triangle\,\lambda_{\text{neighbor}} \end{cases} \tag{3.3}$$

As merit function, just the maximum false classification probability of equation (3.3) is of interest:

$$\text{MF}_3 = \max_{\lambda_i, \lambda_j}\{P_{\text{error}}(g_i, g_j)\}$$

However, the distinction of cases in (3.3) is, on the one hand, not differentiable at the point $|\lambda_j - \lambda_i| = \triangle\,\lambda_{\text{neighbor}}$, on the other hand, the chosen boundary $\triangle\,\lambda_{\text{neighbor}}$ is quite heuristic. The idea is to chose $\triangle\,\lambda_{\text{neighbor}}$ as high as noisy adjacent grey value vectors don't affect the optimization.

3.3   Merit Function to Rate Measurement Uncertainty

Again, equation (3.2) is used to approximate the false classification probability, if two grey value vectors have an overlapping probability density. Ignoring all other grey value vectors beside $\mathbf{g}_i$ and $\mathbf{g}_j$, the assignment $\mathbf{g}_i \rightarrow \lambda_i$ will be perfect with a probability of U. However, according to $P_{\text{error}}(\mathbf{g}_i, \mathbf{g}_j) = (1 - U)$ this assignment will fail. The caused error $\triangle \lambda_{ij} = |\lambda_j - \lambda_i|$ is regarded as measurement uncertainty. The worst case of the solution set S_U:

$$S_U = \{\lambda_i, \lambda_j \in \Lambda, P_{\text{error}}(\lambda_i, \lambda_j) = 1 - U\},$$

is the maximum uncertainty $\triangle \lambda_{i,j}$, which characterizes the CCT senor. This can be optimized using the merit function:

$$\text{MF}_4 = P_{\text{error}}(\arg \max_{\triangle \lambda_{i,j}} S_U).$$

The costs are defined as the probability of false classification for two grey value vectors with maximum distance $\triangle \lambda_{i,j}$ and $P_{\text{error}}(\triangle \lambda_{i,j}) = 1 - U$. This merit function covers both optimality criteria, measurement sensitivity and uniqueness of a measurement. However, due to the maximum operator, the uniqueness property is dominant.

4   Conclusion

A model for the multispectral camera of the CCT sensor is presented. It is used to develop merit functions that can be used to optimize the measurement resolution and measurement uncertainty. The model makes a few assumptions, which require further investigations. Especially, the assumption of a signal with constant shape is quite strict and a series of measurements needs to clarify, if it needs to be relaxed again.

To evaluate the performance of the proposed merit functions extensive optimization calculations are necessary. However, the optimization requires an additional over all strategy, which needs to be developed first. E.g. lokal minima should be handled with an adapted *needle method*, [LM08][FT92]. Further more, it must be investigated if both optimization criteria (resolution and uniqueness) should be optimized simultaneous or successive. Finally, optimization results should be compared with a global optimum, obtained by a complete search. Due to the amount of optimization aspects, it is not possible to discuss the proposed merit functions on its own.

Bibliography

[DHS01] Richard O. Duda, Peter E. Hart, and David G. Stork. *Pattern classification*. Wiley, New York ; Weinheim u.a., 2001.

[FT92] Sh. A Furman and A. V Tikhonravov. *Basics of optics of multilayer systems*. Ed. Frontieres, Gif-sur-Yvette Cedex, 1992.

[JÖ5] Bernd Jähne. *Digitale Bildverarbeitung*. Springer DE, March 2005.

[LM08] Stephane Larouche and Ludvik Martinu. OpenFilters: open-source software for the design, optimization, and synthesis of optical filters. *Applied Optics*, 47(13):C219–C230, May 2008.

[Loe97] Loewen. *Diffraction Gratings and Applications*. Taylor & Francis, May 1997.

[MJ12] Miro Taphanel and Jürgen Beyerer. Physikalisch motivierte mehrdimensionale Farbraum-transformation. In *Tagungsband Workshop Farbbildverarbeitung*, volume 18, Darmstadt, 2012.

[TB12] Miro Taphanel and Jürgen Beyerer. Fast 3D in-line sensor for specular and diffuse surfaces combining the chromatic confocal and triangulation principle. In *Instrumentation and Measurement Technology Conference (I2MTC), 2012 IEEE International*, pages 1072 –1077, May 2012.

Inverse uncertainty quantification of a distributed parameter system: An application for glass forming model

Chettapong Janya-anurak

Vision and Fusion Laboratory
Institute for Anthropomatics
Karlsruhe Institute of Technology (KIT), Germany
janya@ies.uni-karlsruhe.de

Technical Report IES-2012-10

Abstract:
Mathematically, many non-trivial processes involving thermal or fluid transfer can be described as distributed parameter systems. The evolution of a system is governed by *partial differential equations* (PDE), constrained by some boundary conditions. A computer simulation of such an *Initial Boundary Value Problem* (IBVP) allows one to predict the state of the system at different moments in time, and the comparison between the model and observations fixes the model parameters. However, both the prediction and the measurement of a real process are prone to multiple types of uncertainties. In this report we present a concept of the *inverse uncertainty quantification* for a distributed parameter system, useful for identification and quantification of the model uncertainties. First, we build a stochastic model of different types of uncertainties. Next, we perform the *sensitivity analysis* in order to understand their effects on the model and the measurements. Finally, we apply the *Bayesian inference* in order to solve the ill-posed inverse problem of extracting the model parameters and their errors. We illustrate the method with the example of parameter calibration for a glass forming model.

1 Introduction

The computer simulation based on mathematical models now permeates every branch of natural science and engineering disciplines. These mathematical models are derived from physical laws in form of some mathematical equations, which predict the observed values. Since all models are some abstraction of reality, there are always some deviations between the predicted values and the measurements.

These deviations are due to the lack of knowledge and the inherent variability, which can be seen as uncertainties in the model. Uncertainty quantification is the science of quantitative characterization of the uncertainties by using some mathematical tools. For example, the parameter uncertainties in the model can be expressed in terms of some probabilistic model. The model parameters are understood as random variables and the uncertainty is the property of associated probability distribution over their values.

One research topic in the field of uncertainty quantification is the propagation of uncertainty (or propagation of error) which focuses on the influence of the parametric variability on the outputs. The goal is to evaluate the reliability of the model outputs or assess the probability distribution over the outputs. Sensitivity analysis is the study of the effects of parameter variation on system responses. Some sources distinguish these two terms in the way that the sensitivity analysis focuses on apportioned quantification of the impact from different inputs on the predicted model, while the uncertainty analysis describes the entire set of possible outcomes and generally makes no distinction between the different sources of uncertainties.

Another research direction is assessing the cause of the uncertainty given some experimental measurement, or the so called *inverse uncertainty quantification*. It identifies the cause of the output uncertainty and assesses the uncertainty of the source. The goal of the inverse uncertainty quantification is to estimate or calibrate the value of uncertain or unknown parameters of the model, which is also called *parameter calibration* or *parameter estimation*. The other goal is the estimation of the discrepancy between the experiment and the mathematical model called *bias correction*.

In this technical report we explain the general concept of the inverse uncertainty quantification for a *distributed parameter system* (DPS). Mathematically DPS is formulated in terms of *Partial Differential Equations* (PDEs). The general concept of statistical inverse problem for a linear DPS has been discussed in [Ja12]. The concept is extended in term of inverse uncertainty quantification. We demonstrate the inverse uncertainty quantification of a DPS by applying the method to the real industrial glass forming process to calibrate the parameters in the glass forming model.

This paper is organized as follows. In Sec. 2, the background for the uncertainty quantification for the forward as well as for the inverse problem is presented. Sec. 3 shows the application of uncertainty quantification with Bayesian approach to the glass forming process. Conclusions and the directions of future works are presented in Sec. 4.

2   Uncertainty quantification of distributed parameter systems

The word *'uncertainty'* is widely used in many contexts from science and engineering to policy and management. Each field has its own definition and typology of uncertainties based on its purposes as can be seen in various references. However, there is no commonly accepted understanding of the terminology and typology of uncertainties. Accepting the modeller's point of view, we assume the general definition of uncertainty from [WHR+05] as it being *any deviation from the unachievable ideal of completely deterministic knowledge of the relevant system.*

In this technical report the emphasis is on the uncertainty in the DPSs, where the spatio-temporal variability plays an important role. Such systems are common e.g. in biotechnology, chemical engineering, advanced process engineering and manufacturing. A distributed system can be mathematically modeled as an Initial Boundary Value Problem (IBVP) consisting of a Partial Differential Equation or a system of PDEs, Initial Condition (IC) and Boundary Condition. This IBVP can be formulated in general form as

$$
\begin{cases}
\mathcal{D}\left(x(\boldsymbol{r},t)|\boldsymbol{\theta}\right) = s(\boldsymbol{r},t) & \text{(2.1a)} \\
\mathcal{D}_t\left(x(\boldsymbol{r},t=0)\right) = h(\boldsymbol{r}) & \text{(2.1b)} \\
\mathcal{D}_r\left(x(\boldsymbol{r}\in\partial\Omega,t)\right) = b(t) & \text{(2.1c)}
\end{cases}
$$

where $x(\boldsymbol{r},t)$ denotes the system state at time t at position $\boldsymbol{r} = [x,y,z]^T \in \Omega$. The inhomogeneous term $s(\boldsymbol{r},t)$, the system state and its derivatives with respect to time and space are related in (2.1a) by means of some differential operator $\mathcal{D}$. The dynamic behavior and the distributed properties of the system depend on the parameters of the operator, collectively denoted with the vector $\boldsymbol{\theta}$.

In Eq. (2.1b) the operator $\mathcal{D}_t$ denotes a differential operator with respect to time. The function $h(\boldsymbol{r})$ describes the state $x(\boldsymbol{r},t)$ at the entire space $\boldsymbol{r} \in [x,y,z]^T$ at the initial moment in time ($t=0$). Similarly the $\mathcal{D}_r$ in Eq. (2.1c) denotes a differential operator with respect to $\boldsymbol{r}$. The function $b(t)$ describes the state $x(\boldsymbol{r},t)$ at the boundary of the area $\boldsymbol{r} \in \partial\Omega$ for any time t.

The solution of the IBVP is the entire distribution of the state $\boldsymbol{x}(\boldsymbol{r},t)$. From the system theory point of view only some values can be observed, e.g. sensor measurement at some points at some sampled moments in time. These observed values are defined as the system response or the system output. The mathematical interpretation of the system response is the operator R entering the *output equation*

$$y_m = R\left(x(\mathbf{r},t)\right) \tag{2.2}$$

2.1 Sources of uncertainty

The uncertainties are generally categorized as such due to the lack of knowledge or the inherent variability. Furthermore, many authors attempt to further categorize them (e.g. see [KO00], [LvBS$^+$05] and [KD09]). Specifically for the DPS of Eq. (2.1) and (2.2) we categorize the source of uncertainty as:

- *Uncertainties in the model structure*
  A model is an abstraction of the system of interest. Partial differential equations (2.1a) contain some necessary assumptions. In addition, in order to keep the model computable, many simplifications such as linearization of nonlinear models are necessary. Sometimes the system of interest is so complex that no exact structure of models is available. Therefore, the model structure uncertainty always exists, even if all parameters in the model are exactly known. This model structure uncertainty is related to the operator $\mathcal{D}$ in the equation (2.1a).

- *Parameter uncertainties*
  The parameter vector $\boldsymbol{\theta}$ in the Eq. (2.1a) determines the behavior of the state and the model outputs. Often it is difficult to determine the exact values of these parameters, especially in distributed parameter system, where the parameters could be inhomogeneous in the spatial domain Ω.

- *Boundary and Initial condition uncertainties*
  The system of interest has to be separate from its environment. The identification of the system boundaries is not a simple task in general. Interaction between the external excitations and the system state at the boundary is often neglected. Both the system boundary in the spatial and in the time domain and the initial state of the model are difficult to measure or determine exactly. This leads to the uncertainty in the boundary condition and the initial condition in Eq. (2.1b) and (2.1c).

- *Measurement inaccuracies*
  The noise is alway present in measurements, which leads to variability of experimental measurement. There exist also the systematic error. This leads to the uncertainties of the measurement process in the model output Eq. (2.2).

- *Algorithmic uncertainties*
  The IBVP is usually solved with numerical methods such as Finite Element
  Method (FEM) implemented in a computer. Due to numerical approximations, the solution of the model may have discrepancies from the true
  values.

2.2   Forward and inverse uncertainty quantification

The uncertainty quantification is attaching a measure to the uncertainties. It tries
to determine how likely certain outcomes are if some aspects of the system are
not exactly known. The uncertainty can be described using different mathematical
tools (see, e.g. [Mat07]); such as:

- worst-case scenarios

- methods base on fuzzy theory

- evidence theory

- stochastic theory

In this technical report the uncertainties are only expressed with stochastic models.
All quantities in the model are understood as random variables with the associated
probability distributions. Our aim is to identify the probabilistic distributions of
uncertainties. According to the Eq. (2.2), the *forward uncertainty quantification*
is finding the probability distribution of the output y_m from the known probability
distribution of x and other uncertainties in the model. There is a wide variety of
uncertainty propagation methods (for a review see e.g. [LC09]).

In case of the *inverse uncertainty quantification*, unknown probability distribution
of uncertainties in the model are assessed given some experimental measurements.
The general formulation is as follows:

$$y_e(x) = y_m(x, \theta) + d(x) + \varepsilon,$$

where $d(x)$ denotes the discrepancy function and ε denotes the measurement error. The estimation of the discrepancy function $d(x)$ is called *bias correction*. The
estimation of the parameters θ of the model is called *parameter calibration* (or
parameter estimation in some references). These estimations can be done in the
Bayesian framework. In this report we discuss the parameter calibration of a distributed parameter system. For the *parameter calibration* without bias correction
we have

$$y_e(x) = y_m(x, \theta) + \varepsilon \tag{2.3}$$

Estimation of the parameters with uncertainty is equivalent to the estimation of their distributions. Statistical approach for an inverse problem and accordingly parameter estimation under Bayesian framework is presented and discussed in many sources e.g. [KS05], [Jin06], [Lie09] and [NRHP10].

The Bayesian inference combines information from the measurements and the underlying assumptions in the forward model in form of a posterior probability distribution. A posterior probability distribution of a parameter $\pi_{post}(\boldsymbol{\theta})$ is proportional to the product of the prior probability distribution of parameter $\pi_{pr}(\boldsymbol{\theta})$ and the likelihood function $\pi(\boldsymbol{y}|\boldsymbol{\theta})$:

$$\pi_{post}(\boldsymbol{\theta}) \propto \pi_{pr}(\boldsymbol{\theta}) \cdot \pi(\boldsymbol{y}|\boldsymbol{\theta})$$

Provided a prior distribution π_{pr}, the posterior distribution π_{post} can be computed by using *Markov Chain Monte Carlo* (MCMC). This posterior distribution $\pi_{post}(\boldsymbol{\theta})$ provides the values of the parameters, and their uncertainties.

3   Uncertainty quantification of glass forming model

In this technical report we consider the model of the industrial glass forming process [JaBB11]. This is a complex rheological forming process producing glass rods used to preform optical fibers. The figure 3.1 shows the communication flow between the controller and the process. In the controller the model of the process is implemented in order to predict the measurement values. However there are often deviation between the real measurements and the predicted values. In order to adjust the predicted values, the concept of the uncertainty quantification is adopted to calibrate the model parameters, which is discussed in this section.

3.1   Glass forming model

The process setup is visualized in the figure 3.1. The cylinder is fed with a low velocity v_f in an oven where it is heated to its forming temperature. Below the oven the tube is pulled with a higher velocity v_p resulting in thin glass rods (resp. tubes). The process is strongly nonlinear in particular due to the impact of radiation and nonlinear material parameter laws (temperature dependence of the specific heat, effective heat transfer coefficient and the viscosity). In addition, the forming process involves a wide temperature range and large deformations.

Assuming that glass at a high temperature behaves as a Newtonian fluid, the glass flow with free surface can be described with Navier-Stokes equations. Under the

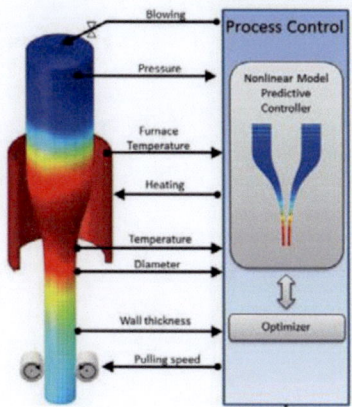

Figure 3.1: Industrial glass drawing process

thin layer flow assumption (which means that the wall thickness or diameter of glass tube is small compared to the length along the axis), the system can be simplified to 3 equations, called *Trouton model* [Loc02].

$$
\begin{cases}
\dfrac{\partial A}{\partial t} + \dfrac{\partial w A}{\partial z} = 0, & \text{(3.1a)} \\[2ex]
\dfrac{\partial}{\partial z}\left(3\mu(T)A\dfrac{\partial w}{\partial z}\right) = -\rho g A, & \text{(3.1b)} \\[2ex]
A\rho C_p(T)\left(\dfrac{\partial T}{\partial t} + w\dfrac{\partial T}{\partial z}\right) - \dfrac{\partial}{\partial z}\left(A\lambda(T)\dfrac{\partial T}{\partial z}\right) = 2\pi R S_r, & \text{(3.1c)} \\[2ex]
S_r = \epsilon\sigma_B\left(T_{oven}^4(z) - T^4(z)\right). & \text{(3.1d)}
\end{cases}
$$

These $A(z,t)$ denotes the cross section area of the glass rod, $w(z,t)$ is the velocity in z-direction, $T(z,t)$ is the temperature of the glass, $\mu(T)$ is the dynamic viscosity, $C_p(T)$ is the specific heat capacity, $\lambda(T)$ stands for the effective heat transfer coefficient (which accounts for the radiative heat transfer in a simple way), $T_{oven}(z)$ is the oven temperature, ρ the density of the glass, g the free fall acceleration, ϵ is the emissivity of the glass and σ_B the Stefan-Boltzmann constant. Eq. (3.1a) represents the mass balance, Eq. (3.1b) the momentum balance and Eq. (3.1c) is the one-dimensional heat transfer equation.

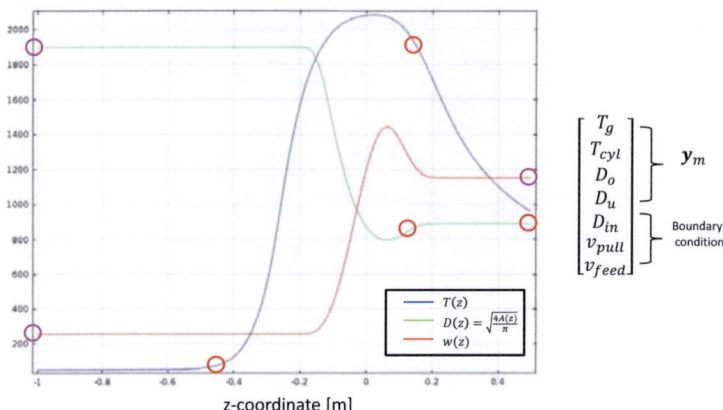

z-coordinate [m]

Figure 3.2: The stationary solution of glass forming process and the illustration of sensors

All three PDEs and their boundary and initial conditions are solved with finite element method. In this report we consider only the stationary case, i.e. the derivative term with respect to time t in the equations (3.1) vanishes. Hence the solutions of IBVP are the distributions $A(z), w(z)$ and $T(z)$ shown in figure 3.2. In real process the measurements are only made at some sensors positions z_{sen}, denoted in figure 3.2 with circles. The measurements with the magenta marks act as a boundary condition, because they represent the parameters of the actuators. The measurement data are compared with the simulation output at the red circle positions.

3.2 Uncertainties in the glass forming model

Because of the lack of knowledge and the model assumptions, there are many uncertainties in the glass forming model, such as the material parameters (C_p, k, and μ), oven temperature profile $T_{oven}(z)$, etc. In this report we focus on the material properties parametrized empirically as

$$
\begin{aligned}
C_p(T) &= a_1 + a_2 \cdot (T[^\circ C] - a_3) \\
\lambda(T) &= b_1 + b_2 \cdot (T[K])^{b_3} \\
\log_{10}\mu(T) &= c_1 + c_2 \cdot \tanh(c_3 \cdot T[^\circ C] - c_4)
\end{aligned}
\tag{3.2}
$$

In this report we assume that the Eq. (3.2) is exact, and consider only the uncertainties of the parameter values. The parameters are modeled as random variables and collected in the parameter vector $\boldsymbol{\theta}$:

$$\boldsymbol{\theta} = \begin{bmatrix} a_1, & a_2, & a_3, & b_1, & b_2, & b_3, & c_1, & c_2, & c_3, & c_4 \end{bmatrix}^\top$$

The parameter vector $\boldsymbol{\theta}$ has 10 dimensions, which is large enough to remember about the *curse of dimensionality*. Thus we will use the sensitivity analysis to capture only the parameters which have more influence on the model, in order to make the computation feasible.

3.3 Analysis of model sensitivity to the material parameters

Calibrating all 10 parameters in vector $\boldsymbol{\theta}$ at once is an unfeasible task. Each parameter has a certain influence on the model. First we identify only the parameter having the most influence on the model using sensitivity analysis as presented in [JaBB11]. Using the method from that paper to the glass forming model in the last section, we get the sensitivity values for entire domain. Considering only the values at sensor position we obtain the values in percent in the table 3.1. It can be seen that the parameters a_2, b_3, and c_3 have more effect compared to other parameters. Therefore we start the calibration with these three parameters as discussed in the following section.

	a_1	a_2	a_3	b_1	b_2	b_3	c_1	c_2	c_3	c_4
$100\% \dfrac{1}{T_g[K]} \dfrac{\partial T_g}{\partial v}$	0.01%	7.26%	0.00%	-0.03%	-0.13%	-3.91%	-0.52%	0.36%	0.52%	0.00%
$100\% \dfrac{1}{T_{cyl}[K]} \dfrac{\partial T_{cyl}}{\partial v}$	-0.01%	5.97%	0.00%	0.42%	0.01%	0.32%	0.00%	0.00%	0.00%	0.00%
$100\% \dfrac{1}{D_u[mm]} \dfrac{\partial D_u}{\partial v}$	0.00%	-1.79%	0.00%	0.01%	0.03%	0.84%	2.53%	-1.52%	-2.59%	0.02%

where v is the parameter in $\boldsymbol{\theta}$

Table 3.1: Sensitivity of values the at sensor positions with respect to parameter values

3.4 Parameter calibration

In this section, we attempt to find the best possible values of the parameters $\boldsymbol{\theta} = \begin{pmatrix} b_3 & a_2 & c_3 \end{pmatrix}^\top$ and their uncertainties by matching to the measurement data. Under the stochastic approach it means that we try to estimate the unknown probabilistic distribution over the random variable $\boldsymbol{\theta}$.

In order to use Bayesian inference as discussed in section 2, we have to fix the forward model of glass forming process, the likelihood function $\pi(\boldsymbol{y}_e|\boldsymbol{\theta})$ and the priori distribution $\pi_{pr}(\boldsymbol{\theta})$.

The glass model Eq. (3.1) and its boundary condition are implemented with the FEM. It is used as forward model, and the solution determines the measurement vector $\boldsymbol{y_m}(\boldsymbol{\theta}) = \begin{bmatrix} T_g & T_{cyl} & D_o & D_u \end{bmatrix}^{\top}$ (see Fig. 3.2) for given each parameter vector $\boldsymbol{\theta}$. Under the assumption of additive white noise with a standard deviation σ of measurements according to the Eq. (2.3), the likelihood function is formulated as follows:

$$\pi(y|\boldsymbol{\theta}) = \exp\left(-\frac{1}{2\sigma^2}\left\|\mathrm{y_m}(\boldsymbol{\theta}) - \mathrm{y_e}\right\|^2\right)$$

Under the assumption that the parameters should lay in some specific interval, the prior distribution of the parameters can be assumed as a uniform distribution. With the likelihood function and the assumed prior distribution, the posterior distribution over the parameters is:

$$\pi_{post}(\boldsymbol{\theta}) = \pi(\boldsymbol{\theta}|\boldsymbol{y}_e) = \frac{\pi_{pr}(\boldsymbol{\theta})\pi(\boldsymbol{y}_e|\boldsymbol{\theta})}{\int \pi(\boldsymbol{y}_e|\boldsymbol{\theta})\pi(\boldsymbol{\theta})d\boldsymbol{\theta}}$$

The posterior distribution can be computed using *Markov Chain Monte Carlo* (MCMC) Method. Based on a Markov chain, the target distribution (or the posterior distribution in our case) is sampled and the state of the chain at stationary state is used as a sample of desired distribution. The resulting chain of the material parameter vector $\boldsymbol{\theta}$ is shown in Fig. 3.3(a). The sample of the chain is plotted in in form of histograms scatter plot as shown in Fig. 3.3(b). These histograms represent the posterior distribution of the parameters.

Together with the scatter plot we can identify the stochastic dependencies of these three parameters. This is the advantage of parameter estimation with the statistical approach over the deterministic approach, which provides only one optimal point solution of parameters not the distribution of parameter. The distribution selects the most probable set of parameters $\boldsymbol{\theta}$ for glass forming model, which is matched to the given measurement $\boldsymbol{y}_m$. The result can be interpreted, that with the parameters from the distribution the glass model will provide $\boldsymbol{y}_m$, which is alike $\boldsymbol{y}_e$ within standard deviation σ.

Without the prior distribution $\pi_{pr}(\boldsymbol{\theta})$, this parameter estimation method is equivalent to the *Maximum Likelihood* method. The prior distribution is normally used to regularize by ill-posed problem. One can see the effects of restricting the values of

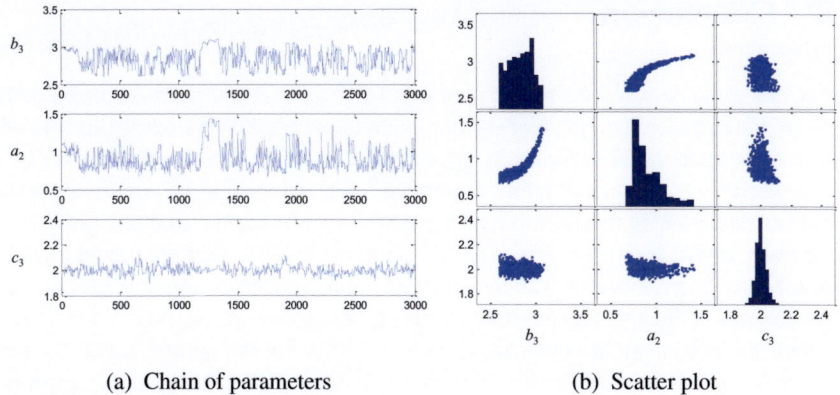

| (a) Chain of parameters | (b) Scatter plot |

Figure 3.3: The posterior distribution of model parameters after the calibration

parameters b_3 and a_2 in Fig. 3.3(b). These restrictions correspond to the specific intervals, which are assumed as uniform distribution in a prior distribution.

As an example, some set of parameters from the posterior distribution is used to simulate the glass forming model. The simulation results are shown in Fig. 3.4. The red circle mark show the output values at sensor position, which are $\boldsymbol{y_m}\left(\boldsymbol{\theta}\right) = \begin{bmatrix} T_g & T_{cyl} & D_o & D_u \end{bmatrix}^\top$. There is a little deviation between the curves but the output values at sensor positions are tolerably identical. For all parameter configurations from scatter plot the deviations between the measurement and the simulation output values at sensor position are always smaller than the accuracy σ of the measurement system.

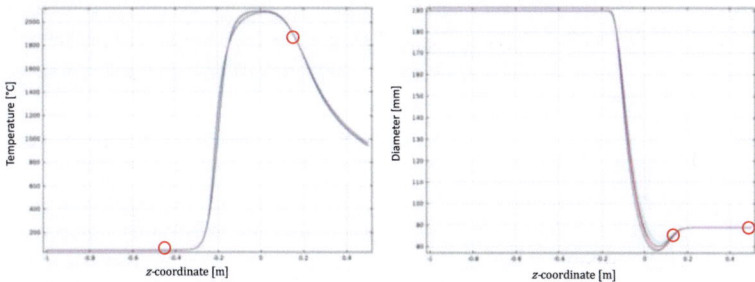

Figure 3.4: Simulation results with parameters from the posterior distribution

4 Conclusion

The deviation between the model prediction and the measurements is unavoidable since it is impossible to possess the complete knowledge of the reality and encode it into the model. The stochastic approach to quantify the model uncertainty is a powerful tool to quantify this ignorance. The dimension of parameter space can be reduced with the sensitivity analysis thus rendering the stochastic approach feasible. In this paper, we apply these techniques to glass forming model in order to calibrate its parameters. The inverse uncertainty quantification provides not just the optimal values of the parameters but the complete probability distributions, which are instrument in improving model's quality. Similar approach may be used to study the uncertainties of the boundary condition, the source term or even the structure of the equation, which will be our future research topics.

Bibliography

[Ja12]   Chettapong Janya-anurak. Statistical inverse problem of partial differential equation: an example with stationary 1d heat conduction problem. Technical report, Vision and Fusion Laboratory, Institute for Anthropomatics, Karlsruhe Institute of Technology (KIT), Karlsruhe, 2012.

[JaBB11] Chettapong Janya-anurak, Hannes Birkhofer, and Thomas Bernard. Numerical sensitivity analysis of a complex glass forming process by means of local perturbations. In *Proceedings of COMSOL Conference*, Stuttgart, 2011.

[Jin06]   Jingbo Wang Ph. D. *BAYESIAN COMPUTATIONAL TECHNIQUES FOR INVERSE PROBLEMS IN TRANSPORT PROCESSES*. 2006.

[KD09]   Armen Der Kiureghian and Ove Ditlevsen. Aleatory or epistemic? does it matter? *Structural Safety*, 31(2):105 – 112, 2009.

[KO00]   Marc C. Kennedy and Anthony O'Hagan. Bayesian calibration of computer models. *Journal of the Royal Statistical Society, Series B, Methodological*, 63:425–464, 2000.

[KS05]   Jari Kaipio and Erkki Somersalo. *Statistical and computational inverse problems*. Springer, New York, 2005.

[LC09]   S.H Lee and W. Chen. A comparative study of uncertainty propagation methods for black-box-type problems. *Structural and Multidisciplinary Optimization*, 37(3):239–253, 2009.

[Lie09]   Chad Eric Lieberman. *Parameter and state model reduction for Bayesian statistical inverse problems*. 2009.

[Loc02]   Horst Loch, editor. *Mathematical simulation in glass technology: With ... 17 tables and 27 videos on CD*. Schott series on glass and glass ceramics. Springer, Berlin and Heidelberg, 2002.

[LvBS+05] Daniel P. Loucks, Eelco van Beek, Jery R. Stedinger, Jozef P. M. Dijkman, and Monique T. Villars. *Water resources systems planning and management: an introduction to methods, models and applications.* Studies and reports in hydrology. UNESCO Publishing, Paris, 2005.

[Mat07] Hermann G. Matthies. Quantifying uncertainty: Modern computational representation of probability and applications. In Adnan Ibrahimbegovic and Ivica Kozar, editors, *Extreme Man-Made and Natural Hazards in Dynamics of Structures*, NATO Security through Science Series, pages 105–135. Springer Netherlands, 2007.

[NRHP10] Cuong Nguyen, Gianluigi Rozza, D. B. Phuong Huynh, and Anthony T. Patera. Reduced basis approximation and a posteriori error estimation for parametrized parabolic pdes; application to real-time bayesian parameter estimation. In L. Tenorio, B. van Bloemen Waanders, B. Mallick, K. Willcox, L. Biegler, G. Biros, O. Ghattas, M. Heinkenschloss, D. Keyes, and Y. Marzouk, editors, *Large Scale Inverse Problems and Quantification of Uncertainty*, Wiley Series in Computational Statistics, pages 151–178. John Wiley & Sons, 2010.

[WHR+05] W.E. Walker, P. Harremoes, J. Rotmans, J.P. van der Sluijs, M.B.A. van Asselt, P. Janssen, and M.P. Krayer von Krauss. Defining uncertainty: A conceptual basis for uncertainty management in model-based decision support. *Integrated Assessment*, 4(1), 2005.

Methods for Multiscale Evaluation of Deflectometric Measurements

Mathias Ziebarth

Vision and Fusion Laboratory
Institute for Anthropomatics
Karlsruhe Institute of Technology (KIT), Germany
mathias.ziebarth@kit.edu

Technical Report IES-2012-11

Abstract:

The perception of defects on specular surfaces is highly dependent on the curvature of the surface and the environment which is reflected in the surface. Flaws can be perceived as disturbances in the curvature. This report gives an overview of methods for multiscale detection and classification of these disturbances caused by defects on the surface. The defects range from large-scale deviations with minimal height like dents or waves to point-like defects like painting defects. For obtaining the geometric data of the surface, deflectometric methods are used. To characterize the surface and to detect deviations from the desired characteristics of the surface several methods based on the wavelet transform are shown and compared with methods in spatial space.

1 Introduction

Specular surfaces are ubiquitous in contemporary design. You can find them on home appliances like toasters, fridges, and washing machines, on furniture, entertainment devices like mobile phones or televisions, vehicles especially on car bodies and many more. In these applications the perception of the surface by a human is of prime importance. There are also cases in which functional aspects are in focus, like rearview mirrors in a car, telescope mirrors, or solar mirrors. In both cases it is not the height of the surface that determines its properties but rather its first derivative. Defects disturb this first derivative and are therefore perceptible or interfere with the functionality. Once a defect is large enough to be resolved it disturbs the aesthetical or functional quality the more the larger its gradient is.

But depending on the application even small gradients can be disturbing, when their extension is large enough. Hence it is important to capture all defects ranging from small to large and assess their severity for the application. Examples mentioned are defects of minimal height like waves or dents and point-like defects like painting defects as blistering. A third application field is the defect detection on technical surfaces. In this case the goal of the inspection may differ from the previously mentioned applications. Thus technical surfaces may be inspected using deflectometry and definitly need to be treated in a multiscale manner but they are not object of this study.

In order to make a comprehensive quality inspection effective, two requirements must be met:

1. A measuring system is necessary that can acquire the relevant geometric characteristics of the surface.

2. An evaluation methodology is required which is able to capture and distinguish different classes of surface properties and defects from the acquired surface data.

Methods based on deflectometry and wavelets are presented that address this problem. Using deflectometric methods to obtain geometric data from the surface, it is possible to meet the requirement of high angular resolution. The problems arising in the measurement of specular surfaces and an explanation of the concept can be found in Section 2. Furthermore, in Section 2.2 methods are shown, that circumvent the deflectometric registration and allow using just a single shot of the surface for defect detection.

To characterize the surface and to detect deviations from the desired characteristics of the surface, methods based on the wavelet transform are introduced. An introduction to wavelets is given in Section 3. Known approaches for the surface characterization and defect detection use mainly features in the spatial domain of the measurement data, e.g., the amplitude of local shape deviations or the amplitude of gradients. Otherwise, features in the frequency domain are used, e.g., for the global assessment of surface roughness. An overview to related work is given in Section 1.1. In contrast, the wavelet transform is a suitable tool to evaluate signal characteristics that extend on both, the spatial domain as well as the spatial frequency domain. For this purpose suitable base wavelets, with features that match the characteristics of typical surface defects, are identified. After using these wavelets for wavelet analysis, methods are introduced to evaluate the wavelet coefficients in the scale space of the wavelet transform in order to detect and classify defects. The feature extraction and classification is described in Section 4.

The methods are designed twofold, first the defects have to be localized on the surface and second they have to be separated into classes.

1.1 Related Work

Depending on the reflectance of the surface, the necessary measurement accuracy and the area of the surface that has to be measured, there are different measurement systems availabe. In this work deflectometry is used to obtain gradient and height information about the surface. Other approaches with completely different measurement systems are related due to similar inspection methods. As this report does not focus on the measurement system some of these approaches are listed below. It has to be considered that the characteristics of deflectometry are high angular precision and a broad range of resolutions.

There are several methods for optical defect detection and classification in spatial space. Nozoe et al. [NSI98] observe the scattering of a laser to inspect silicon wafers. The difficulty in this approach is the high background noise in the measurements made with a laser scanner. For inspection of magnetic disks, Wahl et al. [WSW83] use interferometric measurements. They look for deviations in the interferogram which allows a first assessment of the surface. Especially for the detection of cracks on mechanical parts of a helicopter Fargione et al. [FGPR98] used a microscope to acquire images. For the detection of the cracks a neural network was trained. Another approach by Shima et al. [SKKE86] is to evaluate the gray-level histogram for subareas of the image to find defects. Again Zheng et al. [ZKN02] used a gray-level camera image of a surface and a ring shaped light source to find all kinds of topological defects on metallic surfaces. Therefore, they use a combination of morphological operations and genetic algorithms to learn and detect defects.

In the field of surface metrology wavelets have already been used to describe the statistical properties of the surface, especially surface roughness. While wavelets are used instead of the Fourier transform due to the non-stationary properties of the stastical processes, the studies of Josso et al. [JBL02] and Lee at al. [LZCM98] are not interested in localized properties.

Advanced classification methods and multiscale features like wavelet analysis have been used to find defects on surfaces in the recent years. Zhang et al. [ZDL$^+$11] used the wavelet transform for a smoothing of images taken from a specular surface. The classification is done by a Support Vector Machine (SVM) and based on features taken from spectral measures calculated from a Fourier transform. Ghorai et al. [GMGD12] compared a SVM and Vector-Valued Regularized Kernel Function Approximation (VVRKFA) classifier with features extracted from a discrete

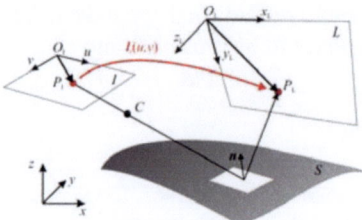

Figure 2.1: Principle of the deflectometric registration from [Wer11].

wavelet transform (DWT) with Haar, Daubechies, Bior and multi-wavelets. They separate the image into small square regions and use the DWT to calculate the energy in each scale which in turn is used to classify each region. Jiang and Blunt [JB04, JSW08] used a stationary wavelet transform (SWT) in combination with complex biorthogonal wavelets. This increased redundancy leads to a better shift and rotation invariance on surface topographies. Li [Li09] used a DWT as prepro-cessing to highlight defects and a SVM to classify regions based on a blob analysis with several extracted features like the area or compactness of the blobs. For im-age acquisition they use a dark field setup. Rosenboom et al. [RKJ11] investigated the use of the wavelet transform with several wavelet families for defect detection on deflectometric measurements.

2 Deflectometry

The problems from inspecting specular surfaces differ from the problems on dif-fuse surfaces. First of all, you can't project any patterns onto the surface and observe them directly. Deflectometric methods are applicable because they use the specularity of the surface. Furthermore, the objective for the inspection depends on the application. If the objective is to find defects that are disturbing for a human, the perception of a human have to be considered. Since the surface itself is mostly visible by its reflection of the surrounding area, the optical aberrations caused by the surface are more perceptible than the surface itself. The virtual image of the surrounding area, which is visible in the specular surface, is determined by its shape or more precisely by its curvature. These curvature information is included in the normal field of the surface. A measurement system as depicted in Fig. 2.1 consisting of a camera with image plane I, a specular surface S as test object, and a screen L is used. A sequence of patterns uniquely coding each point on a screen is observed over the specular surface with a camera. Using these observations, ge-ometric information about the light path from the camera to the screen is obtained in the so-called *deflectometric registration*, which implies information about the specular surface:

$$l : P_I \mapsto P_L, \ l[u,v] = (x_L, y_L).$$

As result of a deflectometric measurement, the deflectometric registration itself can be used as non-metric measurement to characterize the surface and to detect defects, since it can be seen as gradient field of the surface and corresponds to the human perception of specular surfaces. Alternatively the surface can be reconstructed, such that a real metric geometric representation of the surface is available and can be used for the inspection. But without knowledge of the distance between the camera and the surface the reconstuction is impossible. Balzer [Bal08] proposes two approaches to obtain additional regularizing information of the surface that lead to a unique reconstruction. The field was extensivly researched in the past ten years, see [HAN00, LKKH05, SCP05, BSG06, LBRB08, WMHB09, BHWB10].

2.1 Application and Types of Defects

Due to the multiscale nature of the deflectometric principle, it is possible to inspect surfaces ranging from microscopic to macroscopic level. The trade-off one has to make is the lower lateral and angular resolution when inspecting larger areas with the same equipment. The surface material may be made of anything specular or glossy like metal, plastic or glass. A less specular surface with more diffuse reflection lowers the contrast on the screen and therefrom a loss of angular resolution. One way to circumvent this problem is to use a different type of light. For example in the infrared spectrum some materials like brushed aluminum become specular. Generating thermal infrared patterns suitable for deflectometry is challanging, but first approaches have been proposed by Höfer et al. [HWB12]. As deflectometry is applicable to a wide range of materials, there are many practical applications:

- functional surfaces like mirrors

- technical surfaces like cylinder liners in engines

- aesthetic surfaces like car bodies or home appliances

The surface can be characterized globally i.e. by roughness measures or locally by a segmentation of defects. Sometimes it is important to know the location of defects. With this knowledge it is possible to repair the defects locally. For large surfaces like lacquered car bodies this reduces the costs. The following list shows some possible defects on painted surfaces.

- large defects like bumps, dents and waves

- small defects like blistering, corrosion, inclusions, runs and scratches

- texture defects like adhesion loss, bleeding, cracking and orange peel

The defects can be classified further by their shape, origin, or perceptibility.

2.2   One-shot Deflectometry

Most of the defects are already visible in a single image taken with the described setting above and a structured pattern on the screen. They are visible by deformations of the pattern. Detecting those deformations is more complicated for an inspection system than for a human observer. One way to detect those deformations is to suppress the pattern from the screen in the deformed image of the same pattern. Assuming the pattern on the screen is a chessboard pattern, see left image of Fig. 2.2, it can be mathematically described by a one-dimensional grid f using the Dirac delta function δ

$$f(x) = \sum_{m=-\infty}^{\infty} \delta(x + 2m) + \delta(x - 2m - 1),$$

in two directions x and y convolved with a rectangle function Π:

$$f(x, y) = (f(x)f(y)) * (\Pi(x)\Pi(y)).$$

The Fourier transform of $f(x, y)$ is given by

$$F(f_x, f_y) = \frac{1}{f_x f_y \pi^2} e^{\frac{i(f_x + f_y)}{2}} \sin(f_x + 2sf_x) \sin(f_y + 2sf_y).$$

In the frequency domain the pattern is clearly visible, as seen in the right image of Fig. 2.2. As the pattern projected onto the screen is known, the frequency spectrum of this pattern can be used to suppress it in the camera images. Everything that is left over disturbed the original pattern and can therefore be assumed as defect.

3   Wavelets

The wavelet transform is similar to the Fourier transform, as it represents signals in frequency domain. But the Fourier transform is a global transform, meaning that

Figure 2.2: Chessboard pattern in spatial and frequency space.

a local change in the signal affects the whole frequency domain. This is because periodically oscillating trigonometric functions with infinite support are used as base functions. Contrary, the wavelet transform uses small wavelets with finite support both in spatial and in frequency space. This results in a good localization in both spaces. Something similar is achieved with short time Fourier transform with a fixed width window function that is multiplied with the trigonometric functions. Because the size of this window is independent of location and frequency, for short windows in spatial space the localization in frequency space is poor and vice versa for long windows in spatial space. Wavelets have no fixed window length and therefore have a good localization depending for each frequency band. The idea behind the wavelet transform is clear when looking at the calculation of the continuous wavelet transform (CWT). It is defined as the inner product of a signal $f(x)$ with a wavelet ψ in different scalings s and translations t:

$$F(s, u) := W\{f(x)\} = < f, \psi_{s,u} >, \text{ with } \psi_{s,u}(x) = \frac{1}{\sqrt{s}}\left(\frac{x - u}{s}\right). \quad (3.1)$$

In practice the discrete wavelet transform (DWT) is used instead. Additional requirements to the wavelet function assure only dyadic scales and integer translation have to be considered. By defining a scaling function ϕ, the signal $f(x)$ can be approximated in different scales s:

$$a_s[u] = \int_{-\infty}^{\infty} f(x)\frac{1}{\sqrt{2^s}}\phi\left(\frac{x - 2^s u}{2^s}\right)dx, \ (s, u) \in \mathbb{Z}^2.$$

The scaling function has low-pass characteristics, which results in a loss of high-frequency information of $f(x)$ with increasing scale. Furthermore, it is required that the scaling function is orthogonal to the wavelet function, which allows the multiresolution analysis. The wavelet function, which has high-pass characteristics, codes the details that are lost from one dyadic approximation to the next. For an efficient calculation of the approximations and details, instead of the scaling and wavelet function, filter banks are used. Starting with an approximation of the signal in scale s (wavelet crime: $a_0[x] := f[x]$), the next coarser approximation is calculated with low-pass h. The details are calculated with a high-pass filter g. Multidimensional functions are calculated separately in each dimension, resulting in one approximation space and three detail spaces for the 2-dimensional signal $f(x,y)$:

$$a_{s+1}[u, v] = \sum_{m=-\infty}^{\infty} h[m - 2u] \sum_{n=-\infty}^{\infty} h[n - 2v] a_s[m, n], \qquad (3.2a)$$

$$d_{s+1,1}[u, v] = \sum_{m=-\infty}^{\infty} h[m - 2u] \sum_{n=-\infty}^{\infty} g[n - 2v] a_s[m, n], \qquad (3.2b)$$

$$d_{s+1,2}[u, v] = \sum_{m=-\infty}^{\infty} g[m - 2u] \sum_{n=-\infty}^{\infty} h[n - 2v] a_s[m, n], \qquad (3.2c)$$

$$d_{s+1,3}[u, v] = \sum_{m=-\infty}^{\infty} g[m - 2u] \sum_{n=-\infty}^{\infty} g[n - 2v] a_s[m, n]. \qquad (3.2d)$$

One more difference between the wavelet and the Fourier transform is the freedom of choice for the base functions. It is possible to choose a wavelet out of existing families of wavelet functions with special properties or to define a new wavelet. A good overview over the theory and application of wavelets is given by Mallat [Mal09].

Altough the DWT allows a perfect reconstruction of the signal, there has one great disadvantage. By subsampling the signal from one scale to another, more and more information about the signal is lost. This results in a transformation, that depends on the translation of the signal. When the same signal is translated by t the whole scale space may change. It is not translation invariant. By leaving out the subsampling, the undecimated or stationary wavelet transform (SWT) circumvents this problem by introducing additional redundancy. This results in increased memory requirements and increased computational efforts. Nevertheless, the translation invariance is indispensable for the proposed methods.

3.1 Biorthogonal Wavelet

An interesting family of wavelets are the biorthogonal wavelets. They have two instead of one wavelet and scaling function. By defining a separate wavelet for analysis and synthesis, the strict requirement for orthogonality is weakened by a requirement for biorthogonality, which allows new degrees of freedom. The biorthogonality requirement $< \psi_{s,u}, \tilde{\psi}_{s',u'} > = \delta_{s,s'} \delta_{u,u'}$ assures perfect

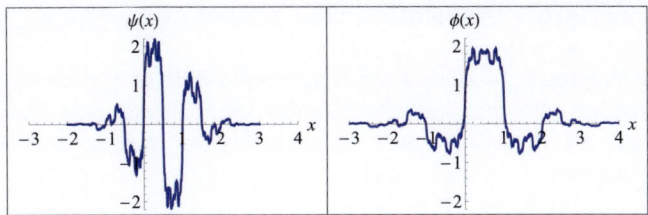

Figure 3.1: Biorthogonal wavelet with five vanishing moments and corresponding scaling function.

reconstruction when using an analysis wavelet ψ and a synthesis wavelet $\tilde{\psi}$:

$$f = \sum_{s,u} < f, \psi_{s,u} > \psi_{s',u'} = \sum_{s,u} < f, \psi_{s',u'} > \psi_{s,u}.$$

The biorthogonal spline wavelet for analysis with five vanishing moments and the corresponding scaling function are shown in Fig. 3.1. It is symmetric around 0.5 which results in a good localization spatial space over all scales. Furthermore, it is orthogonal to polynomials of fourth order due to the analysis wavelet having five vanishing moments. The advantage of this is the nonappearance of coefficients in detail space for curves or surfaces which can be represented by polynomials up to fourth degree. The support length (number of nonzero filter coefficients) of the low-pass is 12, the high-pass has a support length of 4. Let $\mathbf{V}_s$ be the approximation and $\mathbf{W}_s$ the detail space in the scale s spanned by the wavelet and the scaling function. From the orthogonality of the scaling and the wavelet function it follows that the detail space is orthogonal to the approximation space[1]:

$$\mathbf{V}_{s-1} = \mathbf{W}_s \oplus \mathbf{V}_s.$$

The orthogonality of two detail spaces in different scales follows as well. Furthermore, each quadratic intergrable real function can be reconstructed completely from the detail spaces up to scale S and additionaly the approximation space in the scale S:

$$\mathbf{L}^2(\mathbb{R}) = \mathbf{V}_S \oplus \sum_{s=-\infty}^{S} \mathbf{W}_s.$$

---

[1] The operator $\oplus$ denoted the direct sum.

3.2 Correlating Wavelet

Instead of suppressing surface properties, which results in a sparse feature space, one can use wavelets that correlate with the defect classes. The idea is to learn properties of the defects in spatial space and adapt wavelets that match these average properties.

4 Classification

In this section methods to extract features for defect classification in spatial space as well as in scale space are shown. Then parametric and non-parametric classification methods are proposed. Finally covariances within the feature space are investigated.

4.1 Features in Spatial Space

Regarding the image of the surface as signal, defects on the surface g are often high frequency components. A common way to identify them is to amplify these high frequencies. This is similar to an edge filter and can be done by differentiating or high-pass filtering the image.

Linear High-pass   A common way to obtain a high-pass filter is to use a low-pass filter, like a gaussian filter with zero mean and variance σ and subtract the result from the original data.

$$f_{\text{gauss}}(g) = g - g \star \left(\frac{1}{\sqrt{2\pi \cdot \sigma}} \cdot e^{-\frac{x^2}{2\sigma^2}} \right).$$

Non-linear Band-pass   Morphological operators can be used to implement a non-linear band-pass filter. Louban [Lou09] presented two morphological filters to emphasize defects on surfaces. Using simple opening $\circ$ and closing $\bullet$ operators, an appropiate mask S the *Rauh-filter* can be implemented:

$$f_{\text{rauh}}(g) = \frac{1}{2} * (g \circ S + g \bullet S) - g.$$

A similar filter is the *Christo-filter* using two masks. Using mask S_1 for eliminating noise and mask S_2 for eliminating defects the filter is defined as:

$$f_{\text{christo}}(g) = g \circ S_1 - g \circ S_2.$$

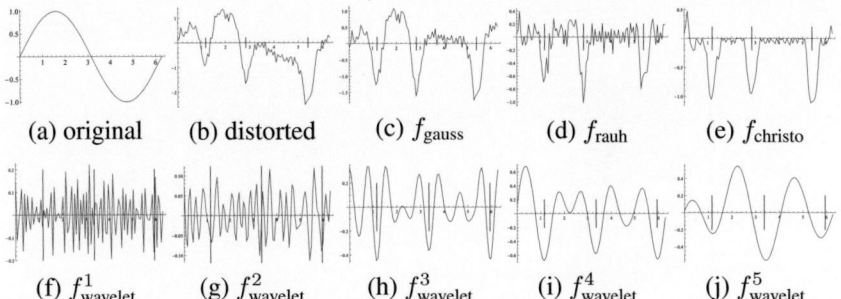

Figure 4.1: Comparison of filters (c)-(j) in spatial space to amplify defects in distorted signal (b) of signal (a).

Spline Approximation   Another way to amplify the defects is to estimate the surface using a spline model. This model should be adjusted to fit the curvature of the surface but not of the defects. It can be regarded as low-pass. Hence the defects are amplified when subtracting this approximated surface $\tilde{g}$ from the data.

$$f_{\text{spline}}(g) = g - \tilde{g}$$

Wavelet Approximation   A common way using the wavelet transform as band-pass filter is to reconstruct the signal using only scale space coefficients of one specific scale. The following Eq. (4.1) is the inverse of the continous wavelet transform as in Eq. (3.1) for one scale s_0:

$$f_{\text{wavelet}}^{s_0}(g) = \frac{1}{C_\psi \sqrt{s_0}} \int_{-\infty}^{\infty} \psi_{s_0,u} < g, \psi_{s_0,u} > du. \tag{4.1}$$

Comparison   Each of the filters in spatial space is highly depend on its parametrization. A graphical comparison using a distorted sinus signal with 3 defects is given in Fig. 4.1. For the wavelet approximation the biorthogonal spline wavelet from Fig 3.1 was used.

4.2   Features in Scale Space

First, a good set of features is needed to describe the surface defects by means of the scale space information. Provided that the coefficients in each scale of the wavelet transform correspond to the data point at the same location, it is possible

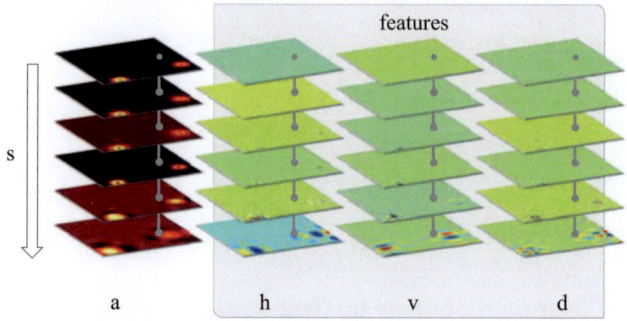

Figure 4.2: The feature vector contains each detail coefficient (horizontal, vertical and diagonal) of the (discrete, stationary) wavelet transform in several scales.

to describe this data point with only the coefficents at the same location. While it is necessary to consider regions of image data in spatial space, each coefficient in scale space is carrying information about the points around it. The size of this surrounding is dependent on the scale.

Depending on the type of wavelet transform, one has to assure the coefficients position at one point match the position of the underlying data point in spatial space. For the calculation of the wavelet transform, see Eq. (3.2), this means, both filter functions have to be symmetric: $h(x) = h(-x)$, $g(x) = g(-x)$.

Using the discrete wavelet transform, the number of coefficients decreases as the scale increases. In contrary in the stationary wavelet transform no subsampling is made, see Section 3. This results in the same number of coefficients in each scale. As a result even coefficients in coarser scales describe only one point in spatial space and any translation directly transfers into scale space without changing the amplitude of coefficients.

For the detection and classification scale and translation invariant features are required. Rotation invariance is less important as long as no isotropic defect structures have to be considered. Another important property feature is the invariance against curved surfaces. When using the detail coefficients of a biorthogonal wavelet and the stationary wavelet transform, the required invariances are met. Hence the wavelet transform has to be calculated in n scales and the horizontal, vertical and diagonal coefficients have to be selected for each point (see Fig. 4.2) and in both directions of the deflectometric registration x_L and y_L:

$$\mathbf{d}^{x_L} = \begin{pmatrix} d_{1,1}^{x_L} \\ d_{1,2}^{x_L} \\ d_{1,3}^{x_L} \\ \vdots \\ d_{n,1}^{x_L} \\ d_{n,2}^{x_L} \\ d_{n,3}^{x_L} \end{pmatrix}, \ \mathbf{d}^{y_L} = \begin{pmatrix} d_{1,1}^{y_L} \\ d_{1,2}^{y_L} \\ d_{1,3}^{y_L} \\ \vdots \\ d_{n,1}^{y_L} \\ d_{n,2}^{y_L} \\ d_{n,3}^{y_L} \end{pmatrix}, \ \mathbf{d} = \begin{pmatrix} \mathbf{d}^{x_L} \\ \mathbf{d}^{y_L} \end{pmatrix}.$$

4.3 Parametric Classification

For the classification a maximum a posteriori decision is made for each point (m, n) on the surface with feature vector $\mathbf{d}(m, n)$ separately:

$$\arg \max_i p(\mathbf{d}|\mu_i, \sigma_i).$$

Tests have shown, that the coefficients can often be assumed as Laplace distributed [ZLGH12]. In consequence the likelihood for class i, represented by the parameter vectors μ_i, σ_i is modelled as univariate Laplace distribution:

$$p(\mathbf{d}|\mu_i, \sigma_i) = \prod_j \frac{1}{\sigma_{i,j} \sqrt{2\pi}} \exp \left(-\frac{1}{2} \frac{|d_{i,j} - \mu_{i,j}|}{\sigma_{i,j}^2} \right).$$

Note that this approach is rather simple, because no covariances between the features have to be learned (Naive Bayes). In practice the product of likelihoods is replaced by a sum of log-likelihoods:

$$p(\mathbf{d}|\mu_i, \sigma_i) = \sum_j \frac{\log \left(\sigma_{i,j} \sqrt{2\pi} \right)}{2} \frac{|d_{i,j} - \mu_{i,j}|}{\sigma_{i,j}^2}.$$

The parameters μ_i and σ_i for the classes *bump*, *pimple* and *error-free* are learned with a training set for each class. The prior is choosen as beeing uniformly distributed, but this could be adapted in practice. If additional prior information $p(\mu_i, \sigma_i)$ is available and necessary a maximum a posteriori decision can be made using Bayes rule:

$$\arg \max_c p(\mu_i, \sigma_i|\mathbf{d}) = \frac{p(\mathbf{d}|\mu_i, \sigma_i)p(\mu_i, \sigma_i)}{p(\mathbf{d})}.$$

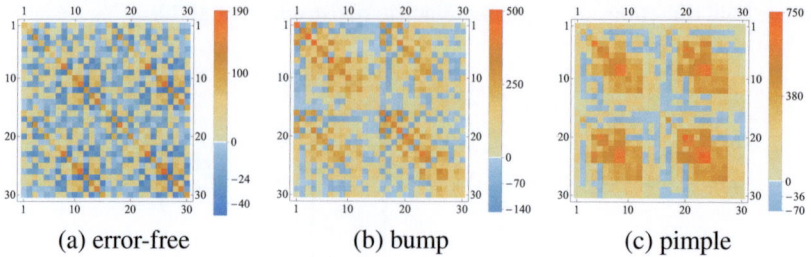

| (a) error-free | (b) bump | (c) pimple |

Figure 4.3: Covariance matrix plots of feature vectors for three classes.

Prior information may be given by an expert, e.g., if only certain classes are possible. Another reason to include prior information is to connect adjacent points on the surface, e.g., it is unlikely that in the middle of a small defect some points belong to a larger defect class.

4.4   Non-Parametric Classification

The approach from the section above can be used with a non-parametric Support Vector Machine (SVM), see [CV95], to determine the likelihood of the feature vectors. For the discrimination of more than two classes, the SVM has to be extended. Chang and Lin [CL11] describe an extension of the SVM to separate multiple classes and additionaly gives probability estimates for each class. Again it is possible to include prior information.

4.5   Investigation of the Feature Space

The orthogonality of the features can be shown theoretically [Mal09, ZLGH12]. By using biorthogonal wavelets this orthogonality is lost. Furthermore, while the orthogonality can be shown theoretically this doesn't have to imply statistical independence of the features. Fig. 4.3 shows the covariances between all features in the feature vector $\mathbf{d}$. While variances on the main diagonals are strongly appearing, the covariances are present enough to falsify the conjecture of statistical independence. As the two directions x_L and y_L of the deflectometric registration are not statistical independent, strong covariances between $\mathbf{d}^{x_L}$ and $\mathbf{d}^{y_L}$ are visible. Hence the covariances within the defect classes 4.3(b) and 4.3(c) are greater than within the feature vectors of error-free regions.

5   Conclusion

This technical report gives an overview of methods for defect detection and classification on specular surfaces. Next to the deflectometric registration, a method was shown to extract information from a single image. The wavelet transform and the family of biorthogonal wavelets was introduced and some important properties were given. Then methods to extract features in spatial as well as in scale space were presented that can be used for the classification. Finally parametric and non-parametric approaches to classify these feature vectors were given and statistical dependencies within the scale space were investigated.

Results of the parametric approach were shown in [ZLGH12] using biorthogonal spline wavelets. Results of the parametric approach using optimized wavelets will be published soon. Results of the non-parametric approach and a use-oriented comparison of important wavelets will be published soon.

Summarizing the wavelet-based approach features a number of advantages against methods in spatial space:

- The classification and defect detection in scale space is easier, since relevant information on surface characteristics and defects is spread on relatively few large coefficients.

- Due to the multiscale nature of the wavelet transform, the detection of both large-scale and small-scale properties is simplified.

- The freedom to choose appropriate wavelets, makes it possible to suppress undesired properties, like the shape of the underlying surface, already in the transformation and not only in the classification step.

This work is financed by Baden-Württemberg Stiftung.

Bibliography

[Bal08]   Jonathan Balzer. *Regularisierung des Deflektometrieproblems – Grundlagen und Anwendung*. PhD thesis, Universität Karlsruhe (TH), 2008.

[BHWB10]   Jonathan Balzer, Sebastian Höfer, Stefan Werling, and Jürgen Beyerer. Optimization on shape curves with application to specular stereo. In *Pattern Recognition – DAGM Symposium*, 2010.

[BSG06]   Thomas Bonfort, Peter Sturm, and Pau Gargallo. General specular surface triangulation. *Proceedings of the Asian Conference on Computer Vision*, II:872–881, 2006.

[CL11]   Chih-Chung Chang and Chih-Jen Lin. LIBSVM: A library for Support Vector Machines. *ACM Transactions on Intelligent Systems and Technology*, 2:27:1–27:27, 2011.

[CV95]   Corinna Cortes and Vladimir Vapnik. Support-vector networks. *Machine Learning*, 20:273–297, 1995.

[FGPR98]   G. Fargione, A. L. Geraci, L. Pennisi, and A. Risitano. Development of an algorithm for the analysis of surface defects in mechanical elements. In *Proceedings of SPIE International Symposium on Intelligent Systems and Advanced Manufacturing Conference*, 1998.

[GMGD12]   Santanu Ghorai, Anirban Mukherjee, M. Gangadaran, and Pranab. K. Dutta. Automatic Defect Detection on Hot-Rolled Flat Steel Products. *Instrumentation and Measurement, IEEE Transactions on*, PP:1–10, 2012.

[HAN00]   Roland Höfling, Petra Aswendt, and Raimund Neugebauer. Phase reflection – a new solution for the detection of shape defects on car body sheets. *Optical engineering*, 39:175–182, 2000.

[HWB12]   Sebastian Höfer, Stefan Werling, and Jürgen Beyerer. Verfahren zur Erzeugung dynamischer Wärmemuster für die Anwendung in der Infrarotdeflektometrie. In *Tagungsband des XXVI. Messtechnisches Symposiums*, 2012.

[JB04]   X. Jiang and L. Blunt. Third generation wavelet for the extraction of morphological features from micro and nano scalar surfaces. *Wear*, 257:1235–1240, 2004.

[JBL02]   Bruno Josso, David R. Burton, and Michael J. Lalor. Frequency normalised wavelet transform for surface roughness analysis and characterisation. *Wear*, 252:491–500, 2002.

[JSW08]   X. Jiang, P. Scott, and D. Whitehouse. Wavelets and their applications for surface metrology. *CIRP Annals - Manufacturing Technology*, 57:555–558, 2008.

[LBRB08]   Jan Lellmann, Jonathan Balzer, Andreas Rieder, and Jürgen Beyerer. Shape from specular reflection and optical flow. *International Journal of Computer Vision*, 80:226–241, 2008.

[Li09]   Te-Sheng Li. Applying wavelets transform, rough set theory and support vector machine for copper clad laminate defects classification. *Expert Systems with Applications*, 36:5822–5829, 2009.

[LKKH05]   Svenja Lowitzsch, Jürgen Kaminski, Markus C. Knauer, and Gerd Häusler. Vision and modeling of specular surfaces. In *Vision, Modeling and Visualization 2005 - Proceedings*. Akademische Verlagsgesellschaft Aka GmbH, Berlin, 2005.

[Lou09]   Roman Louban. Edge detection. In *Image Processing of Edge and Surface Defects*. Springer Berlin Heidelberg, 2009.

[LZCM98]   S-H. Lee, H. Zahouani, R. Caterini, and T. G. Mathia. Morphological characterisation of engineered surfaces by wavelet transform. *International Journal of Machine Tools and Manufacture*, 38:581–589, 1998.

[Mal09]   Stéphane Mallat. *A Wavelet Tour of Signal Processing: The Sparse Way*. Elsevier / Academic Press, 2009.

[NSI98]   Mari Nozoe, Aritoshi Sugimoto, and Takahide Ikeda. Advanced surface inspection techniques for SOI wafers. In *Metrology, Inspection, and Process Control for Microlithography XII*, 1998.

[RKJ11]   Lars Rosenboom, Thomas Kreis, and Werner Jüptner. Surface description and defect detection by wavelet analysis. *Measurement Science and Technology*, 22, 2011.

[SCP05]   Silvio Savarese, Min Chen, and Pietro Perona. Local shape from mirror reflections. *International Journal of Computer Vision*, 64:31–67, 2005.

[SKKE86]   Yoshihiro Shima, Seiji Kashioka, Kanji Kato, and Masakazu Ejiri. An automatic visual inspection method for a plastic surface based on image partitioning and gray-level histograms. *Systems and Computers in Japan*, 17:54–63, 1986.

[Wer11]   Stefan Werling. *Deflektometrie zur automatischen Sichtprüfung und Rekonstruktion spiegelnder Oberflächen*. PhD thesis, Karlsruher Institut für Technologie, 2011.

[WMHB09]   Stefan Werling, Michael Mai, Michael Heizmann, and Jürgen Beyerer. Inspection of specular and partially specular surfaces. *Metrology and Measurement Systems*, 16:415–431, 2009.

[WSW83]   Friedrich Wahl, Samuel So, and Kwan Wong. A hybrid optical-digital image processing method for surface inspection. *IBM Journal of Research and Development*, 27:376–385, 1983.

[ZDL+11]   Xue-wu Zhang, Yan-qiong Ding, Yan-yun Lv, Ai-ye Shi, and Rui-yu Liang. A vision inspection system for the surface defects of strongly reflected metal based on multi-class SVM. *Expert Systems with Applications*, 38:5930–5939, 2011.

[ZKN02]   H. Zheng, L. X. Kong, and S. Nahavandi. Automatic inspection of metallic surface defects using genetic algorithms. *Journal of Materials Processing Technology*, 125–126:427–433, 2002.

[ZLGH12]   Mathias Ziebarth, Tan-Toan Le, Thomas Greiner, and Michael Heizmann. Inspektion spiegelnder Oberflächen mit Wavelet-basierten Verfahren. In *Forum Bildverarbeitung*, 2012.

Karlsruher Schriftenreihe zur Anthropomatik
(ISSN 1863-6489)

Herausgeber: Prof. Dr.-Ing. Jürgen Beyerer

Die Bände sind unter www.ksp.kit.edu als PDF frei verfügbar
oder als Druckausgabe bestellbar.

Band 1   Jürgen Geisler
          Leistung des Menschen am Bildschirmarbeitsplatz. 2006
          ISBN 3-86644-070-7

Band 2   Elisabeth Peinsipp-Byma
          Leistungserhöhung durch Assistenz in interaktiven Systemen
          zur Szenenanalyse. 2007
          ISBN 978-3-86644-149-1

Band 3   Jürgen Geisler, Jürgen Beyerer (Hrsg.)
          Mensch-Maschine-Systeme. 2010
          ISBN 978-3-86644-457-7

Band 4   Jürgen Beyerer, Marco Huber (Hrsg.)
          Proceedings of the 2009 Joint Workshop of Fraunhofer IOSB and
          Institute for Anthropomatics, Vision and Fusion Laboratory. 2010
          ISBN 978-3-86644-469-0

Band 5   Thomas Usländer
          Service-oriented design of environmental information systems. 2010
          ISBN 978-3-86644-499-7

Band 6   Giulio Milighetti
          Multisensorielle diskret-kontinuierliche Überwachung und
          Regelung humanoider Roboter. 2010
          ISBN 978-3-86644-568-0

Band 7   Jürgen Beyerer, Marco Huber (Hrsg.)
          Proceedings of the 2010 Joint Workshop of Fraunhofer IOSB and
          Institute for Anthropomatics, Vision and Fusion Laboratory. 2011
          ISBN 978-3-86644-609-0

Band 8   Eduardo Monari
          Dynamische Sensorselektion zur auftragsorientierten
          Objektverfolgung in Kameranetzwerken. 2011
          ISBN 978-3-86644-729-5

Band 9   Thomas Bader
               Multimodale Interaktion in Multi-Display-Umgebungen. 2011
               ISBN 3-86644-760-8

Band 10   Christian Frese
               Planung kooperativer Fahrmanöver für kognitive Automobile. 2012
               ISBN 978-3-86644-798-1

Band 11   Jürgen Beyerer, Alexey Pak (Hrsg.)
               **Proceedings of the 2011 Joint Workshop of Fraunhofer IOSB and
               Institute for Anthropomatics, Vision and Fusion Laboratory.** 2012
               ISBN 978-3-86644-855-1

Band 12   Miriam Schleipen
               **Adaptivität und Interoperabilität von Manufacturing Execution
               Systemen (MES).** 2013
               ISBN 978-3-86644-955-8

Band 13   Jürgen Beyerer, Alexey Pak (Hrsg.)
               **Proceedings of the 2012 Joint Workshop of Fraunhofer IOSB and
               Institute for Anthropomatics, Vision and Fusion Laboratory.** 2013
               ISBN 978-3-86644-988-6